The Texas Rasslin' War(s) of the 1950s

Greg Klein

Edited by Greg Oliver

Published by OliverBooks
www.oliverbooks.ca

ISBN: 978-1-7378635-2-6 (softcover)
ISBN: 978-1-7378635-3-3 (ebook)

Printed via Kindle Direct Publishing.

Table of Contents

Pro Wrestlers Strike for TV Pay

BULLETIN

SAN ANTONIO, Texas, Dec. 10, (AP)—Ralph "Red" Berry, spokesman for wrestlers appearing in scheduled matches here Wednesday night, refused to enter the ring until television equipment had been removed from the building. San Antonio promoters agreed to cancel the televising Wednesday night but had hopes of reaching an agreement with the wrestlers before next week. The TV station settled for films of matches held earlier in other parts of the country.

HOUSTON, Texas, Dec. 10. (AP)—Thirty-five or 40 wrestlers threatened to strike in Texas Wednesday night unless they are paid television talent fees in addition to a percentage of the gate.

"TV is stealing our talents," Ralph (Wild Red) Berry, a leader of the revolt, announced in San Antonio, Texas. "It's crucifying us. We might as well be wrestling in TV studios. They have no business televising us without our permission."

Berry is supposed to perform in San Antonio Thursday night. But he said he and his colleagues will deliver "an ultimatum" to Promoter Frank Brown if they see a TV camera pointed at them.

Russel A. Hanham, a Houston lawyer, said the wrestlers had engaged him to fight their case in court, if necessary. He attended a meeting of 35 or 40 wrestlers in Dallas, Texas, Tuesday night.

"They are men with brains as well as bodies," Hanham said. "And, boy, are they mad."

"In Fort Worth and Dallas, attendance at wrestling matches has dropped off more than 50 per cent. The wrestlers are paid on a percentage of the house. They blame TV for the drop in attendance."

Berry said he also will deliver an ultimatum Friday night to Morris Sigel, who promotes wrestling in Houston.

"I'm willing to negotiate with them," Sigel said.

But in Dallas, Promoter Ed McLemore said they will either wrestle on TV for him, or they won't wrestle.

"Wrestlers have been well paid for their services here since we started televising the matches," he said. "We enjoyed our best year last year in attendance and total gate receipts, and naturally the wrestlers were paid more for their services than ever before.

"In November, we did our best business in history for that month and, in fact, had the largest crowd in history—more than 7000 paid admissions for one night."

(Berry said that was the night of the presidential broadcasting, when the matches weren't broadcast.)

Feature wrestlers like Berry, McLemore said, make as much as $1000 a performance. He also said he had paid wrestlers up to $500 for TV performances.

The wrestlers appeared to have the support of Texas Labor Commissioner M. B. Morgan, who said the state gets $12,000 to $15,000 a year out of taxes on wrestling and "We would hate to see anything done to hurt our wrestling shows."

"The boys are entitled to some consideration," he said. "Wrestlers have been getting a share of TV receipts in other states. We will look into the situation and see if our department has jurisdiction."

Introduction

"It was all about the TV. McLemore was making money syndicating his show, and the Houston office wanted a piece of it. McLemore didn't want to share, and that's why he broke away and stopped using Houston's talent. He figured he could make it on his own by using and developing his own string of boys. Dallas was a big moneymaker for the Houston office, so going to war was the only logical step."
— Lou Thesz, as told to his biographer Kit Bauman

Despite the song, video didn't actually kill the radio star, but television altered the course of professional wrestling many times. Ultimately, it was the deciding factor in how the business got over to the ticket-buying and match-watching public. Although many wrestling fans and historians know the story about how cable television killed the territory system in the 1980s, fewer people know how national broadcasts almost did the same thing to the business in the 1950s.

This book tells one specific story in that genre although, generally, the story is one that has taken place many times in professional wrestling: A promoter with a good television show gets an advantage over his competitors and uses it to try to expand his business, thus coming into conflict with other promoters.

The Texas Rasslin' War of 1952 to 1954 may have been the first of its kind, but it certainly was not the last territory squabble aided and abetted by television. In a way, the war set the stage for the next four decades of turmoil in the wrestling business, similar but different from infamous cable TV/wrestling struggles known as Black Saturday and the Monday Night Wars. However, in this war, both promotions survived and ultimately, the losing promoter gained a measure of revenge on his rival while he was on his deathbed.

The Texas Rasslin' War of 1952 to 1954 is a story mostly forgotten these days, but it is one that has captivated me since I learned about it a few years ago. This book is an attempt to tell that story, the tale of Morris Sigel and Ed McLemore, promoters of Houston and Dallas wrestling, respectively, and how television turned them from successful partners to bitter rivals.

I grew up a child of divorce and my love of wrestling got enhanced by my parents living in two completely different territories. I lived with my mom in WWF land, where the talk at the bus stop centered on Bob Backlund, Rocky Johnson and Jimmy Snuka. However, my dad lived in Houston, which was an unusual mix of a city-state territory, run by a legendary promoter, Paul Boesch, but associated with Bill Watts and his Mid South Wrestling Association and Universal Wrestling Federation promotions. During two summer visits, my dad took me to the Sam Houston Coliseum, and I am odd enough to think it was one of the biggest blessings of my life. I decided I wanted to be a professional wrestler in the Coliseum on a Friday night in the summer of 1985, a dream I got to live out for a few years in the 1990s. Perhaps more importantly, I started a lifelong love of Houston Wrestling during those Friday nights. That passion led me to the history of Sigel, Boesch's predecessor and mentor. That research led me to the story of the Texas Rasslin' War. My fascination with that

During my brief in-ring career.

story led me to write this book.

As I worked on this project, my view expanded slightly, as I discovered smaller skirmishes in Houston in 1950 and San Antonio in 1959. At that point war became war(s) in my title. By the time I finished writing, I realized I had a pretty good view of Texas Rasslin' in the 1950s, and also an overview of the sport in the state from the beginning to the end of the territory system of professional wrestling in weekly buildings. This expansion brought me in touch with one of wrestling's most infamous con men, Sterling "Dizzy" Davis, with one of the first female promoters, Dorathy Livengood, and her husband Frank Brown, and with Jack Irwin, the liquor store owner from Corpus Christi, who learned about the business the hard way. I also learned about cities and buildings, the Wrestlethon, the Casino Arena, Pappy's Showland, a bunch of Municipal Auditoriums and, of course, the world famous Dallas Sportatorium.

The writing of this book was enhanced by the Jack Pfefer Collection at the Father Theodore Hesburgh Library at the University of Notre Dame. I am grateful to Gregory Bond, the curator of the Rare Books and Special Collections Department, and Holly Welch, the reader services coordinator, and their staff, for their help. An additional thank you to everyone who helped me prepare for the trip and the research.

The world of wrestling historians is small and supportive, so a special thank you to everyone who has helped me, encouraged me and/or inspired me on this project. I apologize if I have left anyone out, but thank you to: Allan Barrie (aka Al Getz), Richard Becerra, Jon Boucher, Jeff Bowdren, Mark Coale, Ricardo Coleman, Jim Cornette, Ian Douglass, Lizzy Flanagan, Steve Gennarelli, Roman Gomez, Beau James, Steven Johnson, Lou Kipilman, Brian Last, John McAdam, Chris McMahon, Tony Richards, Barry Rose, Ray Russell, Cory Santos, Frankie Sechrist, Mike Sempervive, Brian R. Solomon, Shawn Sparks and Karl Stern.

Special thanks to my trainer "Exotic" Adrian Street and mentor "Golden Boy" Jerry Grey for teaching me the inside part of the business.

Another special thank you goes to my editor Greg Oliver, who has always championed my wrestling historian work, and who made this book better.

I'd also like to thank my family for always indulging my love of rasslin' and encouraging me to pursue my efforts to be a part of it and to write about it.

Touchdown Jesus in the background at Notre Dame, home of the Jack Pfefer Collection.

Finally, thank you to all the readers of this book. Together, we are keeping alive the stories of the territory days of professional wrestling. These stories from Texas in the 1950s became a brain worm for me, and at some point last summer, I knew I had to write them into one book and share it with the wrestling world. I hope you enjoy this story as much as I did.

Greg Klein
Cooperstown, New York
@jydbook, @jydbook.bsky.social, @film_greg
April 24, 2026

1
The Players

As the saying goes, there are so many players and personalities who were involved in the Texas Wrestling War(s) that you need a scorecard to keep track. So, here are brief descriptions of the main people involved in the 1950s war.

Morris Sigel (1897-1966)

The grandfather of Houston Wrestling and the Texas circuit, Sigel and his older brother Julius moved to Texas from Manhattan in 1909. They became involved with Houston Wrestling, which listed 1914 as its birth year. Julius took over the business and incorporated as the Gulf Athletic Club in 1925, promoting wrestling and boxing. Morris worked as an accounting clerk for a hardware store, but when he was laid off, he became a full-time promoter with his brother. Julius left the state at the end of the decade to promote Louisiana towns, leaving Morris as the Houston promoter.

The success of Houston Wrestling inspired other promotions throughout the state. Along with brother-in-law Frank Burke and matchmaker Karl "Doc" Sarpolis, Sigel created the Texas Wrestling Agency (TWA) and began booking talent to other cities. Houston became a weekly town in 1930, establishing a 50-year history of weekly Friday night shows. The three men owned a portion of the Dallas wrestling office, too, said to be two-ninths each, with Ed McLemore owning the other third.

"MORRIS GIVES 'EM THEIR MONEY'S WORTH

The cartoon above is an old one, we judge it to be about 25 years old. It was found in a box with more memorabilia of the mat that can only be found near a man who has truly spent his lifetime in the game. Promoter Morris Sigel is that man. If the cartoon was drawn by Sid Van Ulm 25 years ago it would only span half of the career of the man who has promoted longer in one location than any other promoter in any field of sport anywhere in this country, perhaps anywhere in the world!

Plans are underway now to celebrate the Golden Anniversary of Mr. Sigel with an immense show and perhaps a gala and unforgettable series of events. More will be published on that later on as the plans develop but the cartoon above makes it plain that whether it was 25 years ago, or today, Morris Sigel still "gives 'em their money's worth!"

Known for his civic service and good business practices, Sigel promoted Houston Wrestling and the TWA towns for nearly four decades, surviving several attempts by friends and rivals to take his town or territory. He and his colleagues joined the National Wrestling Alliance (NWA) during its first expansion and Sigel served as vice president in 1951. He signed the consent decree with the justice department in 1956; several of his promotional rivals gave testimony.

Sigel discovered, helped develop, or gave an early break to many of the legends in the business, including Gorgeous George, "Nature Boy" Buddy Rogers, Verne Gagne and Antonino Rocca. He and Sarpolis created the Texas title, the top title in the state for nearly 40 years, and the Texas Brass Knuckles title, as well. In addition to Sarpolis, promoters like Ed McLemore of Dallas, Dorathy Livengood and Frank Brown of San Antonio, and Norman Clark of Galveston, another Sigel brother-in-law, developed their towns with Sigel's help. Future Atlanta promoter Paul Jones also worked his way from the ring into the business side in Sigel's Houston office.

Outside of his weekly wrestling shows, Sigel became known for his love of fine art and rich food, the latter often lamented as the source of his health issues. Because Julius died at 47, both Morris and the people around him seemed to think he might also die at a young age. However, he lived until he was 69.

Sigel and his wife Irene had one daughter, Shirley, also known as Lee, married names Steed and then Carriger. Lee also had a daughter, Kim. In the 1960s, Lee was listed as the assistant promoter in Houston, and based on her letters, she seemed to love her father's business and have a good understanding of promoting. She died at age 51 in 1993.

In 1933, Sigel was the first person licensed to promote wrestling and boxing in Texas. Decades later, he was the first promoter to be honored by proclamation by the state legislature. He was known for his philanthropy, for being a fair promoter, and for the impact he had on his protege.

Sigel made Paul Boesch his announcer in the 1940s, first on radio and then on television. Boesch became known as the voice of *Houston Wrestling* and was

Sigel's assistant and protege for nearly two decades. Boesch bought Sigel's Gulf Athletic Club promotion from the Sigel family in 1967, and promoted with various partners for another two decades.

However, Sigel's Dallas rivals finally took over as the state booking office in late 1966, about the same time Sigel became fatally ill.

Edward "Ed" McLemore Jr. (1905-1969)

Starting in the concession stand at the Sportatorium, McLemore worked his way into being a partner and eventual owner of Dallas Wrestling, along with the Texas Wrestling Agency owners, Sigel, Burke and Sarpolis.

McLemore leased the Sportatorium, a 6,400-seat, octagon-shaped building at the intersection of Industrial Boulevard and Cadiz Street. In addition to wrestling, he promoted the *Big D Jamboree*, and both his shows were radio favorites. In 1948, Dallas television gave McLemore the opportunity to expand. He not only booked wrestlers, but was the booking agent for a variety of country music acts. *Big D Jamboree* and *Texas Rasslin'* were shown nationally and both were early television hits, giving McLemore clout and revenue that other promoters did not have. Elvis Presley was among the many performers who appeared at the Sportatorium to join the jamboree.

One of McLemore's proteges was Jack Adkisson, a native Texan who excelled in track and football at Southern Methodist University in Dallas. Adkisson later gained fame as the German heel Fritz Von Erich, and he became a huge Texas star in the 1960s, ultimately abandoning the German gimmick and embracing his roots as a homegrown star, complete with a big babyface turn. Adkisson became McLemore's partner in the Dallas promotion and helped him take over the state booking office in 1966, while Sigel was dying.

Mr. Mac, as many of the boys called him, was also known for philanthropy, in particular with the March of Dimes. His anniversary shows were always fundraisers for that charity, which works to make the lives of the disabled better; every

Ed McLemore Dallas promoter, Sportatorium, Big "D" Jamboree & Texas Rasslin'

SPORTATORIUM GOES UP AGAIN

Symbolizing the start of construction on a new Sportatorium, Promoter Ed McLemore, left, digs a spadeful of earth at the Cadiz and Industrial site. He gets an assist from a friend, Promoter Jack Pfefer of New York City. The old Sportatorium burned down May 1. The new one, costing $150,000 and seating 6,400, will house its first wrestling show in early September.

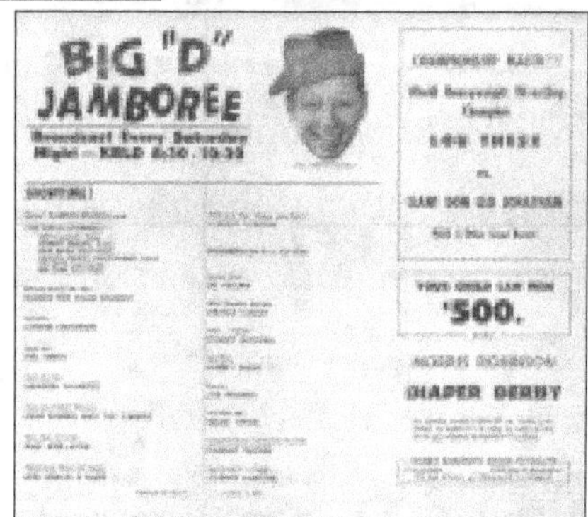

Credits:

1) Dallas Sportatorium program, 1953, courtesy Tony Richards collection
2) Texas Rasslin ad 1955
3) Big "D" Jamboree program featuring wrestling ad, Aug. 3, 1957
4) Dallas News, June 25, 1953 as Ed McLemore & Jack Pfefer break ground on a new Sportatorium

year he made five-figure donations to March of Dimes. He was also known for his Catholic faith.

McLemore and his wife, Rose, had three daughters, and their wrestling office was sometimes a family affair, with the girls working in the office. In times of stress, McLemore was known to refer to his Irish and German heritage, and therefore, he would say, his stubbornness.

McLemore died in 1969, and Adkisson took control of the Dallas promotion and the state booking office, which he operated for more than a decade. His life, and the tragedy of his sons' wrestling careers, are partly captured in the movie The Iron Claw, which took its title from Fritz Von Erich's signature move.

Karl "Doc" Sarpolis (1897-1967)

One of the original "bookers" in the business, Sarpolis changed wrestling by creating many of its innovations.

A football player for legendary coach Amos Stagg at the University of Chicago, Sarpolis studied to be a doctor, but gave up that career for one within the ring. Jack Pfefer lured him into wrestling, portraying Sarpolis as a popular Lithuanian ethnic hero. In 1932, Sarpolis wrestled Jim Londos in front of more than 10,000 people in San Francisco.

As his wrestling days waned, Sarpolis became known for his promotional work. He helped found and did the booking for the nascent Dallas office, and he bought into the Texas Wrestling Agency. He was known for his innovative finishes and creative concepts, such as Lights Out, Texas Death and Brass Knuckles matches. He is credited with developing blading — wrestlers cutting themselves surreptitiously, usually with a razor blade — as a method of getting blood in matches. Often, Sarpolis would travel the Texas loop, working as a special referee in big matches, and the booking office representative behind the scenes.

When Burt Willoughby sold the Dallas promotion, newspaper headlines touted Sarpolis as the new owner. He was a partner, and became the primary

KARL (DOC) SARPOLIS

Matchmaker

Matchmaker for the Dallas Wrestling Club, Karl (Doc) Sarpolis is one of the most well-known men in the wrestling profession, and his personal acquaintance with all the leading wrestling promoters and top-notch grapplers throughout the country enables him to bring to the Sportatorium the very best in mat talent.

Doc can tell you in a flash the record of every wrestler who has been prominent in U. S. mat circles during the last two decades. Only several years ago, Sarpolis was one of the nation's leading heavyweights himself, and today he still boasts a mean body scissors. He has virtually retired from actual competition, but don't let that fact fool you. Doc keeps himself in perfect physical condition and can step in the ring with the best of 'em any time he wishes.

Sarpolis, a college man, is one of the smartest in the game. Broadened by travel, he is a good radio talker and luncheon speaker. He has appeared before luncheon clubs in all the larger cities in Texas to discuss self-defense in the present war crisis, and has given exhibitions of judo wrestling before soldiers in many Texas army camps.

Sarpolis is a top-ranking golfer, and when he's not busy making matches, you'll find him on the nearest golf course beating the fairways in company with several of his wrestler friends.

3,000 SEATS at 50¢ EACH

WRESTLING CASINA ARENA LEXINGTON BLVD. WED., NOV. 18 AT 8:30 P.M.

FOUR (4) MEN GRUDGE TEAM MATCH WITH NEW REFEREE

NATION'S NO. 1 REFEREE DOC SARPOLIS WILL PERSONALLY BE THE THIRD MAN IN THE RING TO SETTLE THIS GRUDGE

PEDRO MARTINEZ — MEXICAN JOE

CAN THESE WIN?

• 2 OUT OF 3 FALLS

TIME LIMIT ? ?

90 MINUTES

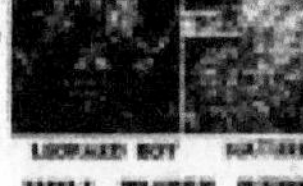

LEONARD ROY — NATURE BOY

WILL THESE REPEAT?

POLICE ON DUTY THROUGHOUT THE AREA – COME OUT AND YELL FOR THE ONES YOU LIKE, AND BOO THE ONES YOU DISLIKE – ANYONE BUT THE ANNOUNCER!

JACK O'BRIEN vs. ROGER McCUNE	RESERVED–$1.00	PHONE 4-5414
JACK KENNEDY vs. BLUE EAGLE	RINGSIDE–$1.50	PROMOTER
BOB O'BRIEN vs. JOHNNY SHAW	GEN. ADM.–50c	JACK IRWIN

Karl Sarpolis And Associates Buy Mat Game

Bert Willoughby, Man Who Revived Pastime Here 15 Years Ago, Steps Out of Picture

Closing out a fifteen-year career as wrestling promoter here, Bert Willoughby has sold out all local interests in the mat game to a group of businessmen represented by W. T. Cox, owner of the Sportatorium, and under the terms of the contract has agreed not to promote sports in Dallas County again within the next five years. A lease for use of the Sportatorium has been made by Cox to the new group for this period.

Cox announced that he was acting only as trustee for the group, whose identity he would not reveal, until they can obtain a charter and form a corporation to be known as the Dallas Wrestling Club. He said four local men were interested in the venture in addition to Karl Sarpolis, veteran Houston wrestler and promoter, who will move his headquarters here and serve as general manager and matchmaker.

Lines Up Big Names.

Willoughby's last show was staged Tuesday night.

Sarpolis, who was largely instrumental in building up interest in wrestling in Houston, said the deal has been hanging fire for several weeks. He has just returned from a trip East for the purpose of lining up several big name grapplers to headline his programs. He said his first show next Tuesday night would feature Ali Baba and he had assurance that within the next few months he would show Gus Sonnenberg, Crusher Casey, Louis Thesz, the Dusek brothers and other headliners of other sections in Dallas.

Confidence in City.

"I am positive," said Sarpolis, "that I can build wrestling up in Dallas to the point where it will outdraw Houston, which for several years has been the best spot in the South. My recipe will be the showing of the best men in the business and giving the fans a real run for their money."

Cox announced that several improvements are to be made in the Sportatorium.

WRESTLING

VINCENT LOPEZ
(Claiming Worlds Title)
vs.
DOCTOR KARL SARPOLIS

MARSHALL BLACKSTOCK
vs.
BOB WAGNER

Monday, October 12th.

POULOS ARENA

Credits:
1) Dallas Wrestling program 1944, Tony Richards collection
2) Dallas Morning-News, Jan. 11, 1939
3) Corpus Christi Caller, Nov. 18, 1953
4) Corpus Christi Times, Oct. 9, 1936

matchmaker until stepping away from the Dallas office briefly in 1953.

In 1952, after Sigel had a stroke and heart attack, Sarpolis attempted to aid McLemore in moving the booking office to Dallas.

Although Sigel recovered and forgave Sarpolis, Doc changed sides again during the Texas Wrestling War. He tried to help promote Fort Worth for the McLemore side, enabled several wrestlers to switch sides and worked as a special referee for big McLemore matches on the insurgent side's circuit.

After the wrestling war ended, Sarpolis left the business for about a year. He bought a hotel, played golf and bided his time, continuing to maintain relationships with NWA power brokers such as Sam Muchnick. When Amarillo owner Dory Detton was having trouble co-existing with his neighboring promoters, Sarpolis bought the territory from Detton for $75,000 in 1955. He took on Dory Funk Sr., an undersized babyface from Indiana who had become a big star in West Texas, as his partner.

In 1936, Sarpolis married his second wife, Vivian, in Sigel's office. Wrestler Ellis Bashara was his best man. He was married three times overall. He had two sons with his first wife Joesphine, both named Karl, as the first boy died as an infant. The second Karl lived a long life. Sarpolis and his third wife, Lucille, had a daughter, Jayne, who was known to work in the Amarillo wrestling office. When she was off at college one year, Sarpolis mentioned it to Pfefer, and in closing said, "I am the office boy now."

After suffering injuries in a boating accident, Sarpolis died in 1967. Dory Funk Jr. and Terry Funk bought his Amarillo shares from his heirs.

Jack Pfefer (1894-1974)

In a business of characters, Pfefer might have been the craziest. An infamous promoter and talent booker, Pfefer was known for outrageous gimmicks, rip-off attractions of famous stars and for scorched-Earth feuds with other promoters. He was despised by many in the business but adored by others, known for

giving gifts and advice. He made stars of Ricki Starr, Buddy Rogers and Jackie Fargo, among dozens of others. A Polish immigrant, Pfefer popularized the ethnic babyface, drawing crowds by featuring a good guy who represented a large group of people.

Pfefer lived in hotels, most prominently New York's Piccadilly Hotel, and his life was a tax deduction. He seemingly kept every piece of paper, thousands of letters, programs, pictures, records and other financial statements, telegrams and envelopes, included.

When Pfefer died, his volumes of correspondences passed to Boston promoter Tony Santos. Santos sold the collection to sports television visionary and Chicago White Sox owner Eddie Einhorn. Einhorn, whose International Wrestling Association group failed in its national expansion attempt in 1975, donated the collection to the University of Notre Dame in 1977.

The Jack Pfefer Collection in the Rare Books and Special Collections section of the Father Theodore Hesburgh Library has 120 cubic feet of Pfefer artifacts, providing research opportunities for wrestling historians that are unrivaled.

Pfefer and Sigel had been friends for decades by the 1950s, including Pfefer having friendships with Sigel's wife, Irene, and daughter, Shirley, also known as Lee. There are at least four decades worth of letters between the two men in the files, filled with personal and professional information.

However, there is a gap in correspondences in the mid-1950s, perhaps because Pfefer was booking talent to McLemore in 1953. Mac and Jack were also longtime friends, and there are also decades worth of connections between the two in the collection.

Pfefer was also good friends with Sarpolis, having started him in wrestling.

Paul "Pinkie" George (1905-1993)

The founder of the National Wrestling Alliance (NWA), George promoted boxing and wrestling. His base was Des Moines, Iowa, and he used his perch to unify Midwestern promoters on a plan for one world champion. In the 1940s, this became the NWA, a cabal of promoters that George ultimately came to regard as a monster he created.

Pinky George

In later years, George got pushed out of his Iowa promotion and became disenchanted with his successor as NWA president, Sam Muchnick. George left the NWA and Iowa and tried to promote various other places, with limited success.

In 1959, George moved to San Antonio and tried to promote against the established promoters. He had help from Morris Sigel and the Houston office, but ultimately focused on a boxing promotion.

"Nature Boy" Thomas Edison "Tommy" Phelps Jr. (1926-2014)

Also known as Izzy Becker, Phelps played one of Jack Pfefer's Buddy Rogers knock offs after Pfefer and Rogers split in 1951. He became a main event wrestler during this run, often working on outlaw and opposition shows.

Phelps was a protege of McLemore's in Dallas and later helped run the Amarillo office for Sarpolis. He was often charged with handling the correspondences. Famously, it is Phelps that first told Pfefer about Jack Adkisson and recommended him for the run where Adkisson becomes Fritz Von Erich. Phelps also wrote to Pfefer frequently in the spring of 1953, sending him clippings, programs and updates on the war in Texas.

Phelps left the business in the 1960s, becoming an early version of a televangelist.

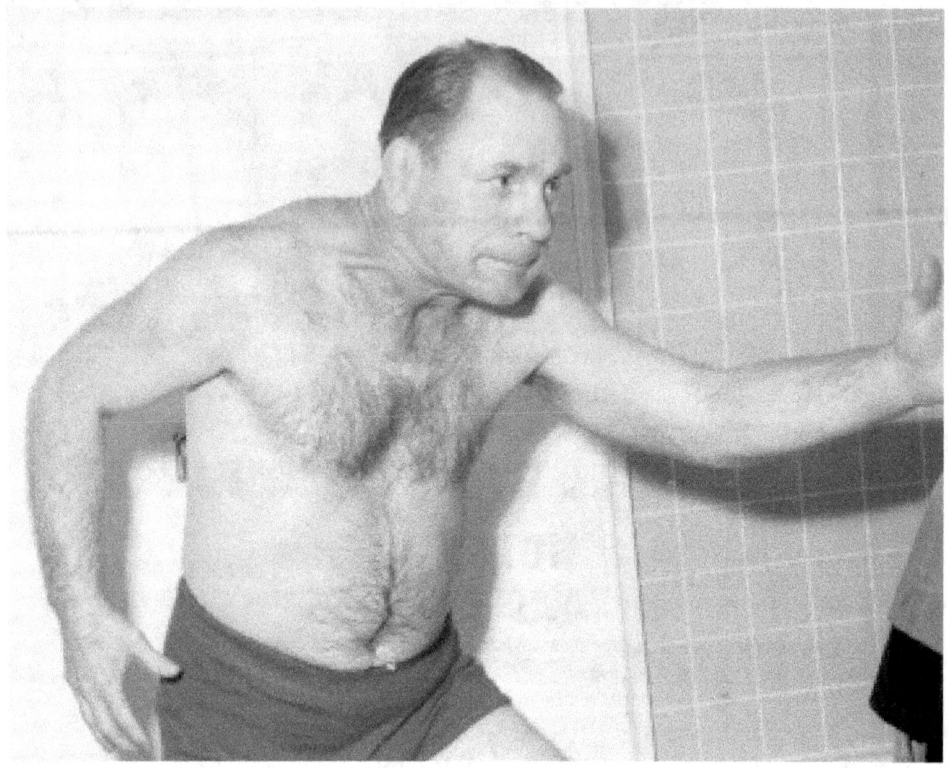

Red Berry. Courtesy Chris Swisher collection

Ralph "Wild Red" Berry (1906-1973)

A top wrestler who became a top manager, Berry was known for revolutionizing the promo part of the business.

Berry started as a boxer, but transitioned to wrestling after breaking both hands fighting. At only 5-foot-8 and just under 200 pounds, he developed his wrestling persona, in and out of the ring, to get attention. Nicknamed "The Mayor of Pittsburg, Kansas" — he had served on his hometown's city council and been acting mayor at times — Berry was a literate villain, condescending and intelligent.

Berry won the NWA light heavyweight title nine times and wrestled from the 1930s into the 1950s.

Berry ultimately settled into a managing role in the WWWF, guiding Gorilla

Monsoon, the Fabulous Kangaroos, Bull Curry and many others. He is credited with recommending Bill Watts to WWWF promoter Vince McMahon Sr., which turned Watts into a Cowboy and set up his career success.

In 1952, when the wrestlers protested the effects of television on live gates and their lack of TV pay, Berry was one of the ring leaders and chief spokesman.

"Dangerous" or "Irish" Danny McShain (1912-1992)

One of the original tough guys in wrestling, McShain started wrestling at 18 and stayed in the business for most of his life, with his peak coming as one of the biggest stars of the 1950s. His brother-in-law, wrestler Donn Lewin, called McShain the "West Coast Buddy Rogers" as McShain was the cocky heel cham-

Danny McShain as a champion.

pion in territories from the deep South to Southern California.

Known for bleeding using the new blading method and for his pencil-thin mustache, McShain was in the first Texas Brass Knuckles championship match in 1953, losing to Bull Curry.

McShain had reigns as the NWA light heavyweight and junior heavyweight champion, including defeating Red Berry for the former title in 1937, and Verne Gagne for the latter title in 1951.

While headlining in Los Angeles, McShain became friends with several movie stars, including Danny Kaye, who started casting him in his films, most notably, *The Inspector General*. At one point, McShain had a contract with RKO Pictures.

In the ring, he was known for the double foot stomp, the Irish Cannonball and the piledriver.

McShain married Sallee Lewin, the sister of wrestlers Mark, Ted and Donn Lewin. They settled in Texas and he stayed connected to the business for the rest of his life, working as a referee for Houston Wrestling. He also sold real estate and did several other jobs, often advertising them in the Houston Wrestling program.

In 1992, his friends and family held a party for McShain that ended with a famous finish so good it may be apocryphal. McShain asked his protege, Tiger Conway, Sr., where they were working that night. Conway told him they were off that night. "Good, because I am tired," McShain said, and he passed away at that time.

In 1952, when the wrestlers protested the effects of television on live gates and their lack of TV pay, McShain was also one of the ring leaders.

Often his name was misspelled McShane. In fact, in press clippings in the 1950s, he is called McShane. The book reflects this awkwardly, quoting the newspapers the way they misspell the name, but correcting it outside of the clippings.

Sterling "Dizzy" Davis (1914-1983)

Also known as Gardenia Davis and Dandy Davis, Dizzy was an innovator of the "gay panic" heel gimmick that later would power the careers of Gorgeous George, Adrian Street and Adrian Adonis. In fact, Davis and George Wagner were friends growing up in Houston, and Davis gave permission to George to use the Gorgeous George gimmick in the United States. The man who played Gardenia in Mexico, was known as a bare-knuckle brawler north of the border. Davis apparently believed the effeminate shtick would not work in America, and told Wagner he could use the gimmick.

Outside the ring, Davis made other questionable decisions. In 1949, Davis tried to start his own Houston promotion. He promised 50% of the gates to the wrestlers, and allegedly had oil-baron backers promising to fund his cause. However, Davis could not get a promoter's license. One of Davis' backers did eventually get licensed, but his promotion could not compete with the established Houston Wrestling.

Chaos and misadventure followed Davis in his post-wrestling life. He sold bulldog-farm starter kits to Texas ranchers, an endeavor that failed spectacularly for the ranchers, and got Davis indicted for fraud. He was convicted but avoided jail because of health issues.

In 1974, Davis hatched a scheme to free his son, Sterling Davis Jr., better known as Blake, but also nicknamed Cooter, from a Mexican prison in Piedras Negras, just over the border from Eagle Pass, Texas. Somehow, the scheme succeeded, freeing Blake and 13 other prisoners. However, it became an international incident, and Blake turned himself in to authorities in Texas. His father and his father's henchmen also went to jail.

By then, Dizzy Davis was known as Dr. Sterling Blake Davis, a practitioner of psychology based on phony credentials.

IT'S GARDENIA (or Dandy) Davis dressed in some of the raiment that has made him known as one of the most colorful grapplers in the light-heavyweight division. Davis acquired the name of Gardenia from his habit of tossing posies to the fair fans at the ringside and the Dandy cognomen resulted from his general aristocratic airs before entering the ring.

Davis meets an opposite type from the standpoint of sartorial makeup when he tackles the bearded, bare-footed Arkansas hillbilly, Farmer Jones, in the Armory feature Wednesday night.

Sterling Davis aka Dizzy Davis aka Gardenia Davis aka Dr. Sterling Blake Davis wrestler, promoter (license denied), doctor of psychology (license from Mexico), bullfrog kit salesman, jail break sponsor

Credits:

1) Arkansas Journal-Gazette, April 4, 1944
2) Houston Chronicle picture from Sterling Davis trial 1976, Greg Klein collection
3) Rockford Morning Star, March 26, 1941
4)High Times, Aug. 1, 1976

Dorathy Livengood and Frank Brown

The husband and wife promoters of San Antonio, Brown was a journeyman wrestler who fell for the older Livengood, who had worked her way up from ticket taker at the Wrestlethon to promoter. They married and ran a successful promotion for more than three decades, featuring weekly matches at their 405 E. Josephine Street arena, the Wrestlethon, which was built for wrestling.

Livengood (1910-1990) famously never watched the matches because she did not leave the ticket booth. Once, Gorgeous George asked her to help him with his hair. Livengood nervously helped the star arrange his locks and was given one of his famous Georgie pins as a reward. However, she anxiously returned to her ticket office afterwards, and said her brief absence left her flustered.

Brown (1913-1977) had begun to crack into main events in Texas in the mid-1940s when he and Livengood became a couple.

Livengood and Brown were the San Antonio promoters for the Sigel/NWA side of the Texas war, and successfully fended off competition from Bob Kline and then Bill Lawlor, who promoted the Municipal Auditorium in turn from April 1953 to early 1954.

At the end of the decade, the couple had a falling out with Sigel, later deemed a misunderstanding. However, San Antonio and Houston ultimately split in 1966 as well. Livengood and Brown promoted shows throughout the south Texas region, ultimately taking over as promoters in Austin, Galveston and several other cities.

In the late 1960s, Livengood and Brown took on a partner, allowing Joe Blanchard, a former Canadian Football League player turned star Texas babyface, to buy into the town. When Brown died in 1977, Livengood sold their shares to Blanchard, who soon after broke away from the Dallas booking office.

It was a Wednesday night at the Wrestlethon in San Antonio, Dec. 10, 1952, that the Texas Rasslin' War began.

Dorathy Livengood San Antonio promoter, Wrestlethon

TROPHY—Dorathy Livengood Brown, the lady rassling promoter, holds the Texas state tag team trophy which will be at stake next Wednesday in a match between Danny Savich and Duke Keomoku, the titleholders, and Rito Romero and the Venezuelan, Anaya.

Iron Man Stunt for Keomoku

Duke Keomoku, the Hawaiian-born Japanese sleeper hold expert, will pull the iron man stunt on next Wednesday night's wrestling show at the Wrestlethon arena, Matchmaker Frank Brown announced Saturday.

The durable matman not only will appear in two matches, one a state championship affair, but also will be in the two main events arranged by the matchmaker. It's possible he may be called on to wrestle a total of six falls.

ONE-HOUR LIMIT

Brown completed arrangements for Keomoku's busy night Saturday when the Japanese agreed to meet Dizzy Davis in a best-of-3-fall main event that will have a time limit of one hour. Keomoku already had been booked with Danny Savich to defend their Texas tag team championship against the challenge of Rito Romero and Anaya, the Venezuelan star.

Davis challenged the Duke for

BIG RASSLE CARD HONORS DOTTIE

Dorathy Livengood will present her 20th Anniversary Wrestling Program next Wednesday at the Wrestlethon Arena. Headlining the big show will be Louis Thesz vs Timmy Geohagen for the N.W.A. Heavyweight toga, and two or three other title frays.

Livengood

It was May of 1930 when the San Antonio promoter got her first taste of promotional wrestling while working for Ralph Hammond. She also worked with Promoter Harry Coffman and after his death completely took over the local scene.

5-Bout Card Likely to Set Crowd Record

Dorathy Livengood, who has taken over the late Harry Coffman's wrestling promotion business for Mrs. Coffman and is making an outstanding success of it, predicted that Wednesday night's show at the Municipal auditorium will set a local record for mat turnouts. Judging by advance sales, the five-bout program will be the most popular, by far, that Miss Livengood and Mrs. Coffman have arranged.

Photo credits:

1) San Antonio Light, April 22, 1951
2) San Antonio Express May 12, 1950,
3) San Antonio Light, July 12, 1944, early mention as Livengood takes over San Antonio promoting

Frank Brown, wrestler, San Antonio matchmaker, promoter

FRANK BROWN

SAN ANTONIO
THE LIGHT

4-D SAN ANTONIO LIGHT Sunday, April 11, 1948.

Gal Promoter Throws Hubby To Mat Lions

Brown Gets Main Event Mat Chance

Likeable young Frank Brown is going to get his first San Antonio wrestling main event opportunity Wednesday night at the Municipal auditorium when he tackles George "K. O." Koverly in the feature attraction of Promoter Harry Coll-man's wrestling card.

Brown has been waiting a long, long time for this opportunity. Five years ago, when his mat career was just beginning to blossom, Brown suffered a puzzling knee injury, and he was forced to lay off for four years.

Credits:

1) San Antonio Evening News, Sept. 14, 1959
2) The San Antonio Light, June 23, 1950
3) The San Antonio Light, April 11, 1948
4) La Prensa, March 15, 1944
5) The San Antonio Light, June 14, 1945
6) The San Antonio Light, March 15, 1944

Thur. June 14, 8:30 p. m.
— DOUBLE MAIN EVENT —
DAVE LEVIN vs.
BOBBY MANAGOFF
2 out of 3 falls—1-hour limit.
FRANK BROWN vs.
BUDDY ROGERS
2 out of 3 falls—1-hour limit.
DUTCH SCHULTZE vs.
MARVIN JONES
WRESTLING
Ticket Sale, Auditorium, G-7491
PRICES: 60c, $1.08, $1.65
Enlisted Men 33c

LUCHAS
Auditorio Municipal
HOY a las 8:15 p. m.
"K. O." Koyerly
VS.
Frank Brown
PRECIOS DE ENTRADA:
40c — 75c — $1.10

THIS WEEK ENJOY

TELEVISION'S BIGGEST AND BEST SHOWS

Dennis Day	Favorite Story	Your Hit Parade
Kate Smith	Life of Riley	Private Secretary
You Bet Your Life	The Ruggles	Fred Waring
Racket Squad	Toast of the Town	Red Buttons
Texas Rasslin'	Arthur Godfrey	Front Page Detective

And Many Other of Your Favorites

17-Inch Wayne

199.95

RCA VICTOR is 5 ways finer

(1) Improved "Magic Monitor"
(2) Improved "Deep Image"
(3) New Automatic UHF-VHF Tuner
(4) New Long Distance Reception
(5) New Wider Range of Cabinets

Ask about an RCA Victor Factory-Service Contract covering complete television installation and service by electronic experts of the RCA Service Company. Available only to RCA Victor owners.

269.95

339.50

369.50

399.50

399.50

439.50

SPRAGINS CO.

818 Scott Street — Phone 3-2721

Credits:

1) Ad, Times Record News, May 31, 1953, Wichita Falls, Tx, including Texas Rasslin' as one of the popular shows

2

Television

"If wrestling changed during the '50s, then television played the role of accelerating the change. If wrestling drew bigger houses in some area than had ever been attracted before, the television most certainly shares the applause. But there is another side to the story, and television must share the blame for a number of failures."

— Paul Boesch, in his autobiography,
Hey Boy! Where'd You Get Them Ears?

While movies had been popular in America and other countries since early in the 20th century, television didn't develop fully until the 1940s, and it didn't catch on until after World War II. However, during the post-war era, TVs became ubiquitous in American households. Color television in the 1960s, cable television in the 1970s and video cassette recorders in the 1980s advanced the technology.

Jan. 1, 1949, the new year in Houston began with the first broadcast by the first local television station, KLEE. According to Paul Boesch, the first two shows on the station were *The Milton Berle Show* and *Houston Wrestling* with Paul Boesch. Wrestling was a perfect show for television; it was relatively inexpensive to produce, easy to light and shoot, and featured endless stories and episodes to entertain viewers.

In a 1981 anniversary retrospective published by *The Wrestling News*, Boesch wrote: "With the start of 1948, I took on a new assignment as a member of Morris Sigel's staff. I did a radio broadcast, from ringside, of some of the matches. I was not exactly a stranger to the microphone. In 1936, in Portland, Oregon, I was interviewed between falls in the main event. The announcer, Rollie Truit, handed me the microphone when the wrestlers returned to the ring and said, 'You broadcast the next fall.' I stammered a protest, but he walked away and I became a radio announcer.

Paul Boesch early in his career on the radio. Crown Studios Collection, Alexander Turnbull Library

"I became a television announcer in much the same way. I did the radio broadcast for KLEE for a full year. At the end of that year, W. Albert Lee had the license for Channel 2 and had a television station ready to go on the air. In the first week of January 1949, I did my first telecast. I hadn't even seen television and suddenly I was on it!

"For the first nine months of telecasting we started with the 'Star Spangled Banner' and wound up when the lights went out. It is difficult to explain, 33 years later, when people are blasé and bored with the miracles the tube produces, that the early days were exciting. It is hard to explain how people stood in front of TV sets placed in store windows to watch wrestling; and how Friday night was a wrestling party night in someone's home."

In North Texas, WBAP in Fort Worth went on the air in the fall of 1948.

Dallas station KRLD debuted in spring 1949, with *Big D Jamboree* and *Texas Rasslin'* becoming two of its mainstays.

The Texas State Historical Association, in an article on the *Big D Jamboree*, wrote: "Just after World War II, in addition to his wrestling promotions, McLemore began presenting a weekly country music variety show on Saturday night at the Sportatorium. The show, originally christened *The Texas State Barn Dance*, and then renamed *Lone Star Jamboree*, eventually in 1948 became *Big D Jamboree*, broadcast from the Sportatorium on KRLD. The Saturday night shows would continue until 1966. By the early 1950s, the show had also secured a slot as one of the revolving Saturday night national broadcasts on CBS radio.

"During the 1950s, the Sportatorium played host to an impressive lineup of country and rockabilly performers, and later, stars of the new genre of rock-and-roll. Guests included both local talent and up-and-coming stars. Hank Snow, Hank Williams, the Light Crust Doughboys, Carl Perkins, Johnny Carroll, Wanda Jackson, Johnny Cash, Ronnie Dawson, Elvis Presley, and many others, graced the stage, along with Jamboree regulars such as Charline Arthur, Sonny James, Hank Locklin and Helen Hall."

The *Texas Rasslin'* show had similar success. Announced by Ves Box, and later Maurice Beck, the show aired in Dallas and was also syndicated across the United States and into a few international markets. It featured the Texas Wrestling Agency wrestlers in their Dallas-specific feuds. Although it was not as renowned as the Dumont Network show from Chicago or the NWA Hollywood matches, *Texas Rasslin'* lasted longer — into the 1960s — and had a wider reach thanks to the international markets.

In San Antonio, the first television station, KOAI, signed on Dec. 11, 1949. Soon after, it was airing pro wrestling from the Wrestlethon, the house that wrestling built, and where Livengood and Brown promoted.

Wrestling thrived in Texas in the post-war era. The circuit established by Sigel, Burke and Sarpolis included Monday nights in Fort Worth at the North Side Coliseum, Tuesday nights at the Sportatorium in Dallas, Wednesday nights at

Credits:
1) Texas Rasslin' Ad, The Billboard, May 28, 1955

the Wrestlethon in San Antonio, Thursday nights at the Town Hall in Corpus Christi and Friday nights at the City Auditorium in Houston. Saturdays were spot shows. The Texas Wrestling Agency wrestlers often did spot or weekly shows on other nights, too. Sundays were dark because of religious "blue laws" that prevented sports and entertainment activities on the Sabbath.

In 1953, the Associated Press ran a small story on wrestling in Texas, quoting figures from the Texas Department of Labor. From September 1952 to September 1953, there were 31 weekly towns, and 43 total towns, grossing a total of $1,761,801, or close to $21 million by 2025 money. "The biggest wrestling

HOUSTON VS DALLAS

All-Out 'War' Seen In Texas Wrestling

DALLAS, Dec. 26, (AP)—The grunt and groan boys are at it again in Texas, the Dallas News said tonight.

The newspaper reported an all-out wrestling competition war is in prospect for Dallas and may eventually spread over the state.

The News said it learned that Ed McLemore, local wrestling promoter, will have competition from his former allies, the men who operate the Texas Wrestling Agency out of Houston.

Here is the newspaper's report:

The Houston group plans to stage matches on Tuesday nights, in direct competition to McLemore's weekly show here.

McLemore plans to stage two shows a week, adding a Thursday night program to his regular Tuesday night performance. He will be denied the services of wrestlers furnished him in the past by the Texas Wrestling Agency but will import talent himself.

McLemore said tonight the struggle between rival wrestling promotions may spread over the state.

The trouble began in a dispute over the distribution of television receipts. A group of wrestlers recently refused to go into the arena at San Antonio until television cameras had been removed; the wrestlers said they would strike unless given a share of the television take.

McLemore, whose matches have been carried "live" locally and on TV film over the nation, contends that he has contracts with the wrestlers furnished by the Houston agency and that the contracts cover the subject of television rights.

He threatened to go to federal court if necessary, with the allegation that the Houston agency is conspiring to bring about a violation of those contracts.

Frank Burke, a partner in the Houston agency with Promoter Morris Sigel, told the News by telephone tonight that his group "hopes to open" in Dallas Jan. 6.

Credits:
1) Corpus Christi Caller, Dec. 27, 1952

city in Texas is Houston," the article read. "For the second straight year, promoter Morris Sigel guided the sport to its biggest box office year, according to the *Houston Chronicle*."

The timeframe used to measure the business includes nine months of the wrestling war, so some cities have two promotions, either going head-to-head with shows (Dallas), or staggering shows on different nights (Corpus Christi, San Antonio). Dallas actually had three shows for a good portion of the war. Also, the Amarillo territory is running shows under the banner of founding promoter Dory Detton, so not all of the towns are Texas Wrestling Agency or Southwest Sports Agency (McLemore) towns. El Paso, the sixth biggest city in Texas in 1950, had its own promotion and circuit as well. However, it is clear wrestling in Texas in this era was indeed big business. The TWA loop included six of the top seven biggest cities in Texas, according to the 1950 Census: (1) Houston, 2) Dallas, 3) San Antonio, 4) Fort Worth, 5) Austin and 7) Corpus Christi. None of them used the outdoor stadiums, yet, or had million-plus populations like the biggest cities in the country — Houston with about 600,000 residents was the 14th largest city in the United States in 1950; Dallas at 22nd was smaller than New Orleans, Buffalo and Baltimore. Incidentally, 70 years later, the Texas cities dominate the top 20 list, according to the 2020 census, with Houston (4th), San Antonio (7th), Dallas (9th), Fort Worth (11th) and Austin (13th) all representing.

Many of the markets thrived as wrestling towns long before television. Some like Dallas and Houston had radio wrestling shows. Radio seemed to enhance attendances but television turned out to have the potential to harm the business. As soon as wrestling debuted on television, a new term and concept entered the lexicon of wrestling promoters: giving too much away. The problem isn't hard to understand. Television itself was popular. Suddenly, people could sit at home and be entertained by moving pictures. When wrestling became televised, it became a popular television show and it made it easier for fans to watch the matches, but it also made it easier for them to not pay to watch the matches in the arena.

Boesch's nephew and 1980s co-promoter Peter Birkholz Jr., wrote in the book *When Wrestling was Rasslin'* that Sigel's Houston promotion initially suffered box office decline when television caught on. However, *Houston Wrestling* quickly stopped showing the main events, and later edited the television shows to be unofficial advertisements for the next week's shows. As Birkholz wrote: "Attendance at the matches was dropping and *Houston Wrestling* fans decided they could stay at home and not buy tickets. That was not good news for Morris Sigel, who not only made his money at the gate, but also at the concession stands. Wrestlers were also concerned since their compensation was based on box office receipts. Sigel moved the telecast to 10 p.m. on Friday nights and did not televise the semi-finals and main events. This was the beginning of the strategy wrestling promoters would use for the next four decades. They used television shows to 'tease' and live wrestling shows to 'please'."

In his autobiography, Boesch noted the switch to cutting off main events had to be explained wrestling style. "If Morris Sigel would forbid the telecast of those two matches, after so many months of permitting it, he would soon assume the role of an ogre, somewhere between Scrooge and the Devil himself," he said. Instead, McShain, as the bad-guy champion, refused to have his matches televised, telling the fans they had to pay to see him wrestle. "Yet, Danny's decision, based on it was on financial reasoning, was honest," Boesch wrote. "Like all main eventers, he wrestled on a percentage of the house. Television was cutting into the gate and he was taking home less in his pay envelope. It was simple economics."

The first over-saturation of wrestling on television happened quickly, with shows catching on nationally from Hollywood, Chicago and Dallas, in addition to local-market shows. The money from television rights went to the promoter, and were not often, if ever, being shared with partners or the wrestlers.

Historian Tim Hornbaker noted the NWA's 1952 convention had a notable argument between Sigel and McLemore over the television rights and receipts from *Texas Rasslin'*.

McLemore claimed he approached Sigel and his partner, Frank Burke, with the idea of filming the matches, and they turned down his offer. So, he started a new company without them, and signed the wrestlers to exclusive contracts to ensure they would not disappear from his shows.

The contracts became part of the issue, but so did the money, of course. McLemore later said he made $60,000 just in 1952 from the licensing of Texas Rasslin'. By the end of the year, Sigel and his associates were claiming they had been cheated.

McLemore suspected Sigel's response was a plot to control the airwaves. In a Nov. 28, 1952, letter to Jack Pfefer, McLemore alleged Sigel met with Los Angeles promoter Johnny Doyle in Houston on Nov. 15, to plot out a nationwide takeover. "I found out today what they are trying to do to me. Sigel and Doyle have been together in a meeting and I have it on good authority from the west coast. They are starting a movement to smother the promoters on the TV end of the game and hog it all for the Booking Offices of a select few of the Czars. Unless a lot of the promoters around the country wake up and do something about it pretty quick, they might get the job done."

Seemingly, nothing came of the meeting, and Doyle had a worse 1953 than any of the Texas war figures, losing his Los Angeles promotion and seeing his marriage fall apart in tabloid-like fashion, as his wife Kathryn alleged cheating, abuse and alcoholism, and the Los Angeles papers ran with the story. Ironically, the person who tried to help his failing promotion in 1954 was Doc Sarpolis, who for all his cunning, seemed to choose sides unwisely.

So, there were pre-existing bad feelings between Sigel and McLemore heading into the December showdown in San Antonio, and when the lawyers arrived this time, the lawyer for Houston Wrestling was there to help the wrestlers with their claim.

In San Antonio, the Livengood/Brown promotion caught on quickly to the television problem, and newspaper reports state San Antonio TV never aired the main events or other top matches from the arena shows. However, that did not prevent San Antonio from being in the eye of the storm. TV depressing live attendance was a subject the 100-plus contracted wrestlers in Texas had been discussing for much of the early 1950s. In late 1952, the boys were getting angry about the situation. On Tuesday, Dec. 9, at the Sportatorium in Dallas, the wrestlers met and their anger turned to action. The main event between McShain and Ricki Starr drew a disappointing crowd. It should be noted that some newspaper accounts, and promoter Ed McLemore, disputed the crowd was down, but it is indisputable that the boys were angry. Newspaper accounts state 35 or

Pro Wrestlers Strike for TV Pay

BULLETIN

SAN ANTONIO, Texas, Dec. 10. (AP)—Ralph "Red" Berry, spokesman for wrestlers appearing in scheduled matches here Wednesday night, refused to enter the ring until television equipment had been removed from the building. San Antonio promoters agreed to cancel the television Wednesday night but had hopes of reaching an agreement with the wrestlers before next week. The TV station settled for films of matches held earlier in other parts of the country.

HOUSTON, Texas, Dec. 10. (AP)—Thirty-five or 40 wrestlers threatened to strike in Texas Wednesday night unless they are paid television talent fees in addition to a percentage of the gate.

"TV is stealing our talents," Ralph (Wild Red) Berry, a leader of the revolt, announced in San Antonio, Texas. "It's crucifying us. We might as well be wrestling in TV studios. They have no business televising us without our permission."

Berry is supposed to perform in San Antonio Thursday night. But he said he and his colleagues will deliver "an ultimatum" to Promoter Frank Brown if they see a TV camera pointed at them.

Russel A. Bonham, a Houston lawyer, said the wrestlers had engaged him to fight their case in court, if necessary. He attended a meeting of 35 or 40 wrestlers in Dallas, Texas, Tuesday night.

"They are men with brains as well as bodies," Bonham said. "And, boy, are they mad."

"In Fort Worth and Dallas, attendance at wrestling matches has dropped off more than 50 per cent. The wrestlers are paid on a percentage of the house. They blame TV for the drop in attendance."

Berry said he also will deliver an ultimatum Friday night to Morris Sigel, who promotes wrestling in Houston.

"I'm willing to negotiate with them," Sigel said.

But in Dallas, Promoter Ed McLemore said they will either wrestle on TV for him, or they won't wrestle.

"Wrestlers have been well paid for their services here since we started televising the matches," he said. "We enjoyed our best year last year in attendance and total gate receipts, and naturally the wrestlers were paid more for their services than ever before.

"In November, we did our best business in history for that month and, in fact, had the largest crowd in history—more than 7000 paid admissions for one night."

(Berry said that was the night of the presidential broadcasting, when the matches weren't broadcast.)

Feature wrestlers like Berry, McLemore said, make as much as $1000 a performance. He also said he had paid wrestlers up to $100 for TV performances.

The wrestlers appeared to have the support of Texas Labor Commissioner M. B. Morgan, who said the state gets $40,000 to $50,000 a year out of taxes on wrestling and "We would hate to see anything done to hurt our wrestling shows."

"The boys are entitled to some consideration," he said. "Wrestlers have been getting a share of TV receipts in other states. We will look into the situation and see if our department has jurisdiction."

Texas Rasslers Demand TV Cut

BY UNITED PRESS

HOUSTON, Dec. 10. — Professional wrestlers in Texas, who have "brains as well as bodies," threatened Wednesday to walkout on their mat performances if they don't start getting a cut of television receipts as well as their share of actual gate receipts.

The matter was disclosed by Attorney Russel A. Bonham, who returned Tuesday night from a meeting of matmen in Dallas.

Bonham, attorney for Promoter Morris Sigel here, said about 35 wrestlers attended Tuesday night's meeting and "boy are they mad."

"In Fort Worth and Dallas attendance at wrestling matches has dropped off more than 50 per cent," Bonham said. "The wrestlers are paid on a percentage of the house. They blame TV for the drop in attendance."

Bonham said the wrestlers, headed by Ralph (Wild Red) Berry, were threatening to strike at Wednesday night's bouts in San Antonio.

Credits:
1) Beaumont Enterprise, Dec. 11, 1952
2) San Antonio Evening-News, Dec. 10, 1952
3) M.B. Morgan, Commissioner. Bureau of Labor Statistics

40 wrestlers were part of the meeting, although normal cards had 10 or 12 wrestlers at work. McShain, the NWA World Junior Heavyweight champion, and "Wild" Red Berry, an articulate heel who had also been the junior world champion, took the lead, rallying the wrestlers to take action on the television issue.

Wednesday, Dec. 10, in San Antonio, the wrestlers did take action. According to the United Press International, the group invited an attorney, Russell A. Bonham — the Houston lawyer who represented Morris Sigel and the Texas Wrestling Agency — to attend the meeting. Via Bonham, the wrestlers issued a press release Wednesday before the matches. They telegraphed their intention to strike in San Antonio unless they got their share of television pay or the cameras were turned off and no matches were filmed.

According to the article, Bonham said about 35 wrestlers attended Tuesday night's meeting. "Boy are they mad. In Fort Worth and Dallas attendance at wrestling matches has dropped off more than 50 percent," Bonham said. "The wrestlers are paid on a percentage of the house. They blame TV for the drop in attendance."

"TV is stealing our talents," Berry said in another article. "It's crucifying us. We might as well be wrestling in TV studios. They have no business televising us without our permission."

"I'm willing to negotiate with them," Sigel said in the article.

McLemore is quoted saying the opposite. "Wrestlers have been well paid for their services here since we started televising the matches," he said, noting the wrestlers will work his television or will not work for him. "We enjoyed our best year last year in attendance and total gate receipts, and naturally, the wrestlers were paid more for their services than ever before."

Berry and McLemore traded accusations about the attendance figures. McLemore: "In November, we did our best business in history for that month and, in fact, had the largest crowd in (Dallas) history, more than 7,000 paid admissions for one event." Berry responded by pointing out the record crowd was drawn on a night, Tuesday, Nov. 4, where the matches were not televised.

Instead, the network focused on the presidential election.

Once the wrestlers arrived in San Antonio, they sent Berry to speak with the promoters, Livengood and Brown. They had telegraphed their intentions with the newspaper articles that day, but Berry made it clear. If the television cameras were there, the wrestlers would not be there. The San Antonio promoters reportedly called Sigel in Houston and were told to acquiesce to the wrestlers' demands. The television cameras were removed. By most accounts, KOIA showed a movie that night instead, although at least one newspaper account said an old wrestling program was repeated. Either way, the matches took place as advertised in San Antonio on Dec. 10: Juan Humberto defeated Ike Eakins by count out. Berry and Cyclone Anaya wrestled a 20-minute time-limit draw. Gory Guerrero beat Duke Keomuka by disqualification. Andre Drapp and Jack O'Reilly wrestled a 20-minute time-limit draw. In the main event, McShain successfully defended his title against Billy Varga.

Although the show went on, the trouble still brewed. In a *Houston Post* story the next morning — headlined "Wrestler's demands to be met if reasonable, declares Sigel" — Sigel said he, too, would meet with the wrestlers and he did not anticipate any trouble. "Wrestlers have always enjoyed a part in television monies in Houston, and I believe their demands are something to be negotiated," he said.

"The problem up to this point is mainly a Dallas issue," Sigel continued. "The Dallas market has been saturated with televised wrestling, both live in Dallas and Fort Worth and on film from out-of-state points. The wrestlers are not threatening to strike against television but only on the point that they should share in the television monies."

The wrestlers sent a letter to Sigel stating their case. "Our purses are figured on a percentage of the gate and with television and filming cutting down the gate, because people can sit at home and see the matches anyway, it is hurting our income and our only source of living," the *Post* quoted from the letter. "We can't be blamed for wanting to protect our only source from which we make

Wrestlers Win Point, to Get TV Cut

Local Situation Still in Doubt

[illegible]

Issue Clouded

[illegible]

"Looks like they meant what they said 'about striking for TV pay, here in San Antonio."

Rattlers Start Longest Road Trip

[illegible]

Rasslers' Demands Halt Live TV Mat Shows for S. A.

Live wrestling on television will be suspended in San Antonio until difficulties can be ironed out between the wrestlers and the promoters.

Wednesday night wrestlers refused to ply their trade at the Wrestlethon until TV cameras had been removed.

Ralph "Wild Red" Berry, spokesman for the matmen, said the wrestlers were "sick and tired of wrestling before half-filled houses, half-filled because of television, and we're not getting one penny from television although the shows carry sponsors."

Frank Brown, local matchmaker, summed it up this way:

"The move by the wrestlers is not what it seems on the surface. They are not demanding TV receipts as supposed. The brunt of the attack is directed against filming of TV wrestling to be shown in cities all over the country at a later date. These films have become the wrestlers' stiffest competition and they are hurting their earnings more than anything. The TV receipts from live wrestling is a small part of the picture. Actually, here in San Antonio, we already are cutting them in on the receipts."

The focal point of the attack is Dallas and the general concession is that other cities were included because no one could be singled out.

Brown added that matches at the Wrestlethon would continue to operate normally, but TV would be suspended until things are ironed out.

Next Wednesday's matches will be the final ones of the year and Brown hopes difficulties can be ironed out during the Christmas holidays.

M'Shane Wins

Danny McShane successfully defended his junior heavyweight title against Billy Varga Wednesday night, but received a severe tongue-lashing from Referee Lew Voss in the process.

In winning the first fall, McShane twice caused Varga to go sailing over the top rope, a procedure which generally causes disqualification at the local arena. However, Voss allowed the two grapplers to proceed and McShane used a series of [illegible] to take the fall in [illegible]. Voss followed the champion to his dressing room and warned him about the disqualification rule and threatened to disqualify McShane out of his title if he repeated the foul.

EVENS COUNT

Varga made short work of "Dangerous Dan" in the second fall and used whips into the turnbuckles and a flying head scissors to even the count in just 3:27.

Varga continued domination of the champ in the third fall and finally hit the air with his clincher, a flying head scissors. But McShane had other ideas. He turned the scissors into a jack-knife that held for the 3-count in 13 flat.

Fans were treated to one of the fastest matches of the night in the semi-final as Andre Drapp and Australian Jack O'Reilly went 20 minutes to a draw after attempting almost every hold in the books.

Voss was on the warpath again when he disqualified Duke Keomuka after only 2:27 of the top preliminary and awarded the match to Gory Guerrero. The Duke caught Gory on the ropes repeatedly and slashed him with repeated judo chops to the throat. Finally, after Voss had given the order to break several times, the Duke accidently cut Voss across the chest and the Jap was disqualified. Voss relinquished his official status and connected with a deep kick to the Duke's mouth. Police intervened at the request of Frank Brown and Voss hurled match challenges at the Duke.

BERRY GETS DRAW

Cyclone Anaya and "Wild Red" Berry fought to a 20-minute draw, but Berry refused to accept the decision. Voss called for a voice-vote from the fans and Anaya was the fans' choice as Berry received one lone vote. The official verdict of a draw stood, however.

In the opener, Juan Humberto was given the decision when Joe Eakin was unable to return to the ring in the 30-second time limit.

Credits:

1) San Antonio Light, Dec. 12, 1952
2) Editorial Cartton, Dec. 10, 1952
3) San Antonio Light, Dec. 11, 1952

our living." The letter was signed by Berry and McShain, as well as Anaya, Ellis Bashara, Guerrero, Ray Gunkel, Keomuka, Otto Kuss, O'Reilly, Starr and Varga — basically, all main eventers at the time.

"I am ready to make any reasonable concession the wrestlers are entitled to," Sigel said. "I think television can be the greatest of all mediums, if properly handled. It can be mishandled. I think an excellent job has been done in Houston."

If the implications weren't already abundantly clear, the *Post* drew the distinction in the next paragraph, explaining the Dallas promotion had other ideas. "No wrestlers will be used here who will not agree to have their matches televised," McLemore said.

From the beginning, Karl "Doc" Sarpolis appeared to be caught in the middle. He was the booker in Dallas and owned two-ninths of the Dallas promotion. However, he was also one-third owner of the Texas Wrestling Agency. He and McLemore had tried to take over the state booking office earlier in the year, following Sigel's stroke in June, but Sarpolis expressed empathy for the wrestlers. "No wrestler is opposed to televising his match, but he does want to share in the proceeds," Sarpolis said.

The next day the state of Texas got involved in the form of Texas Labor Commissioner M. B. Morgan. There was no television in Corpus Christi on Thursday but there was lingering anger among the boys and growing tension between the promoters. Instead of heading south to Corpus Christi or to other bookings, Berry and McShain took a detour from San Antonio and drove 80 miles north to the state capital in Austin.

Monta Brown Morgan (1890-1958) had served three terms in the state legislature, as a House member from Grayson County, about an hour north of Dallas. Gov. Beauford Jester appointed Morgan as a department head in 1947, and Morgan continued to serve in that post after Jester's death in 1949. Morgan served in his position for more than 11 years, until his death in 1958; he was succeeded by his wife, Katherine.

Critics derisively referred to Sigel as the "czar" of Texas Wrestling and often suggested Morgan was his lackey. Like Sarpolis, Morgan seemed to be playing to the middle of the television dispute. He issued a statement after the meeting Dec. 11, saying he felt the wrestlers were justified in seeking their share of television money. However, he said he did not approve of the sudden strike and warned the wrestlers they could lose their licenses if they refused to honor their contracts.

Berry and McShain went on to their matches and the wrestlers' concerns were addressed and not addressed respectively by the Houston and Dallas contingents. Morgan declared the labor part of the situation tentatively resolved, with no strike, and a path forward for the wrestlers' concerns to be addressed and their livelihoods protected.

San Antonio's Frank Brown told his city's paper his version, and framed it in a way that pointed to the argument at the NWA convention between the promoters. "The move by the wrestlers is not what it seems on the surface," Brown said. "They are not demanding TV receipts as supposed. The brunt of their attack is directed against the filming of TV wrestling to be shown all over the country at a later date. These films have become the wrestlers' stiffest competition and they are hurting their earnings more than anything. The TV receipts from live wrestling are a small part of the picture. Actually, here in San Antonio, we are already cutting them in on the receipts." Brown said TV would not air until the dispute had been resolved. The show ran again in the new year.

The next paragraph in the story is not attributed or a quote, but it is telling: "The focal point of the attack is Dallas, and the general consensus is other cities were included, because no one could be singled out." The other cities saw it for what it was. "Houston vs. Dallas," said a Corpus Christi version of the Dec. 27, 1952, story from the *Dallas News* about the aftermath of the almost strike in San Antonio. "All Out 'War' Seen in Texas Wrestling."

December 1952 ended with articles of declaration but with no battles fought. However, everyone knew. A Texas-sized wrestling war loomed.

3

Dizzy's War

Before going forward with the story of the 1953 Dallas vs. Houston war, it is worth looking back at another battle fought by the Houston Wrestling promotion, formally known as the Gulf Athletic Club.

As Morris Sigel established Houston as a wrestling town, two complementary things happened to turn city-level success into the Texas loop through East, North, Central and South Texas. The wrestlers that worked in Houston on Friday nights needed places to work Monday through Saturday. The success of the Houston promotion inspired promoters in other Texas cities to stage their own matches. The Texas loop started in 1930, at the same time Sigel made his town a weekly town.

In late 1929, when Sigel announced his intentions to promote nearly weekly, promoters in San Antonio and Corpus Christi announced plans to do the same. Fort Worth and Dallas charted similar paths in the early 1930s. However, it is more than the main cities that developed during the 1930s. A wrestler that worked Thursday in Corpus Christi, for instance, could also work that week in Rio Grande Valley cities Harlingen, McAllen, Brownsville and Laredo. Or, at Houston area shows in Beaumont, Galveston and Port Arthur. Or, northeast of San Antonio at shows in Austin, Killeen and Seguin. Or, at shows in any number of cities in the Dallas-Fort Worth area. Or, they could work at shows in any combination of the main and spot towns, any week of the year. By 1936, when the Dallas Sportatorium opened on Industrial Boulevard at Cadiz Street, the Texas loop looked like it would look for the next 50 years, a profitable circuit of wrestlers and towns that reportedly grew to 140 contracted performers in 30-plus towns in the 1950s.

However, the money had a siren's call, which more people heard than just the officially licensed promoters. The history of wrestling is filled with stories of wrestlers who thought promoters took too much of the money. Or, with promoting partners who believed they would be more successful if they cut the other partners out of their shares. Or, with promoters who were sure they would be more profitable if only they did not have to pay a booking fee to the office. Or, with wrestlers who were sure they could make bigger money working for a different promoter, or knew they could make more money if they were the promoter.

Sigel's biggest star, the Depression Era hillbilly hero Leo Daniel Boone "Whiskers" Savage, real name Edward Civil (1899-1967), became such a sensation he won a version of the world title in 1935 when he was basically still a rookie. Houston was arguably Savage's biggest town and Sigel and his matchmakers played a huge role in turning the mountain man into a famous attraction. The storyline gimmick sold Savage as a simple man who could not wrestle. He couldn't even afford wrestling gear, so he wore overalls, or jeans held up by a rope belt. He showed up with pet dogs, chickens and possums. However, the mountain man was the best fighter in the world.

Decades later, a feature on Sigel noted he had an office filled with wrestling memorabilia, but a house filled with fine art. The exception was a picture of Savage in his home. When asked why he placed the mountain man among the art, Sigel replied, Savage was the reason he had the house and the art. When Sigel was ailing or warring in the 1950s, Savage always returned to lend a business hand or moral support. The promoter and his biggest star became lifelong friends and Savage died less than two weeks after Sigel.

Count Billy Varga, star of movies and wrestling, wrote Jack Pfefer to tell him the news Feb. 15, 1967. "You remember Savage. He made Sigel a lot of money."

Yet, in 1937, Savage and Sigel got into a dispute. Savage no-showed a card

Whiskers Savage. Department of Special Collections, University Libraries of Notre Dame

where he was supposed to defend his world title against Little Beaver and was stripped of the title and suspended. This wasn't a wrestling storyline. Savage disappeared from Houston cards and didn't return until after the dispute had been settled in 1938. The fans wanted their hero back, Sigel wanted his biggest star back and Savage wanted to headline in one of his best towns again, instead of being badmouthed there in the press and by the promoter. They worked it out, and Savage became Houston's biggest star, perhaps ever, but certainly before the late 1960s, when Wahoo McDaniel arrived.

Again, disputes like these exist throughout the history of wrestling. Even friends sometimes get sideways with one another. And not everyone is friends to begin with, or, to end with. Because of the nature of the game, business associate is a more apt term for the relationships between wrestlers and promoters, between wrestlers and other wrestlers, and between promoters and their peers. Even if the competition in the ring is not real, the battles outside the ring were legitimate.

Houston native Sterling Davis was a main event star in Texas and in Mexico. In Mexico, he had success giving out flowers and he caused a stir as a suggestive, gay-panic heel character. In the United States, he kept the elaborate robes and charismatic look, but passed the rest of the gimmick onto George Wagner, his childhood friend who would become Gorgeous George. In Texas, Dizzy Davis was a crazy fighter. He was a rival of Houston transplant Danny McShain and they helped pioneer double-juice matches, where both wrestlers bled to get over the danger of the action. Houston/Dallas matchmaker Doc Sarpolis often was the third man in the ring for these kinds of events.

Wrestling historian Tony Richards, whose biography on Dory Funk Sr. has had him probing all things about Sarpolis and the Funks' Amarillo territory, had a couple of thoughts on Doc, both as the third person in the 1953 war, and the third person in the wrestling ring.

"Doc was a master manipulator," Richards said on Episode 75 of *Greg Klein's Old School Rasslin' Talk*. Richards even characterized Funk Sr.'s 1973 manipulation of the NWA title switch — which was supposed to be Dory Funk Jr. dropping the title to Jack Brisco, but ended up being Junior dropping the title to Amarillo favorite Harley Race — as Senior doing "that Doc Sarpolis shit" with Funk Jr. claiming to have been hurt on the family farm. By the way, Episode 13, "The Farm Accident Heard Round the World" is the most popular episode of *Greg Klein's Old School Rasslin' Talk* podcast, since it dropped, and seemingly forever. However, Episode 78, "Escape from Piedras Negras" about Dizzy Davis and the jail break has begun to challenge that status. The master manipulation — the Doc Sarpolis shit — was a skill obviously passed along to the Funks, and the 1973 Umbarger, Texas, farm accident is one of wrestling's great history mysteries, something still compelling more than a half century later.

So, Sarpolis as a special referee was for more than storyline. A normal referee

Another Fashion Plate!

Southern Californians, gradually pulling themselves together after going through one of the hottest political campaigns in history, are due for another stormy siege.

Sportsdom's zaniest headliner, Dizzy Davis, is set to launch his particular virulent brand of fireworks in the wrestling circles.

Vainer of his "manly beauty" and exotic robes than a peacock, Davis predicts that his dazzling appearance is going to make Gorgeous George and Lord Blears quite drab in comparison.

Daffiest of all the razzle-dazzle boys, Dizzy is a terrorist of the madman variety — but there's a definite method in his zaniest tactics as the spectators are going to find out early.

One of the biggest box office attractions in matdom throughout the East, South and Midwest for many years, Dizzy is the type of star who's earnestly hated by the fans—who nevertheless turn out by the thousands for his every appearance, in the hope (usually in vain) that he'll be blitzed.

He's been in plenty of trouble on the mats and with the fans has the newcomer from Texas—but to date, has weathered some terrific storms, emerging with a series of wins over all kinds of tough opposition.

Dizzy, who is as notorious for his sensational attire as he is for his infamous mat practices, has earned for himself, however, a big name as a designer throughout the world.

Bill Stern, sports commentator, in a recent national broadcast, recently credited Dizzy Davis with designing some gorgeous materials used by the President of Mexico for his own dressing gowns!

So apparently, Davis' dizziness pays off—and well.

He could make a huge fortune in the field of design, but Davis isn't content to settle down to what he says is a more or less should be almost invisible unless the action calls for something dramatic, such as cheating behind the referee's back, or a disputed pinfall. In reality, a referee is a part of every match, and good ones help in all ways mental and many ways physical. A special referee, by definition, has a higher storyline purpose, provided to control the action between wrestlers when things have previously gotten out of control. The tough, athletic Doc, who fought Strangler Lewis seven times, according to one newspaper article, was the perfect man for that gimmick and set the script for it in the business, as Sarpolis played the role as far back as the 1930s. "This is another innovation by Doc Sarpolis," Richards said, "where the booker and matchmaker refs the main event, so he can call spots for the guys and even change the finish if he thinks the crowd is reacting in a certain way and the return could draw better than originally planned. The most significant booker who used this innovation was Leo Garibaldi, who had some famous match and finish changes when he was refereeing a main event."

In July 1950, Sarpolis refereed a series of matches between McShain and Davis that built on events outside the business for a year, and ended up running in Houston's City Auditorium for three weeks, counting the surprise challenge.

The McShain-Davis rivalry had an unusual buildup.

On Feb. 27, 1949, Davis cracked his breast bone in a match in Oklahoma City. The injury kept him out of action for about three weeks. He had a side business installing neon signs and a fair amount of business contacts in Houston, but he also had a wife and three small children, so there were certainly some financial concerns. This seems to be the point where Davis decided he wanted to be a wrestling promoter, or at least, when he got serious about his desire to be a wrestling promoter.

In the spring, he filed an application with the Texas Department of Labor for a promoter's license in Houston. Davis announced a plan to pay the wrestlers 50% of the gate. He had rumored financial backers, including a local oil baron. He planned to run at the Olympiad Auditorium, where owner Hugh Benbow had been a boxing promoter, a rival to the Sigels, and had recently rebuilt his venue to host the Junior Olympic trials (and a roller skating palace). Benbow would go onto greater fame as manager and mouthpiece for Cleveland Williams. A three-round knockout loss to Cassius Clay in 1966 actually gave Williams a boost, career wise, in part because of his brash, slick-talking manager, who mocked Clay (later known as Muhammad Ali) and predicted victory for his protege, the Big Cat. The Olympiad sat 8,000 fans, twice as many as the City Auditorium, where Sigel ran. With a business grudge against Sigel and a newly upgraded facility at 2418 Center St., Benbow was the perfect partner for Davis, as he took a shot at the Houston establishment.

The state of Texas had other ideas. In June, the Texas Department of Labor held hearings in Austin, presided over by Commissioner M.B. Morgan. Davis had a lawyer for him and two against, one from Dallas and one from Houston. He would deem the state to be against him, too. However, the ultimate decision to deny Davis a license came down to his own crimes, before and during the hearing.

According to a *Houston Chronicle* article July 1, 1949, Bonham represented the Houston office, while Dallas had Aubrey Roberts representing their organization, the Wrestling Organization of Texas. Seymour Lieberman of Houston represented Davis.

Lieberman focused much of his case on the three-year binding contracts Sigel and the TWA issued, trying to make the hearing about the conditions on the circuit for the boys.

The other lawyers had a case to make about Davis. After denying his intention to operate a booking office, he admitted to contacts with other cities, promoters and venues. Curiously, TWA co-owner Sarpolis was mentioned as offering support, and a venue in the Dallas-Fort Worth area if things worked out.

The Houston and Dallas attorneys questioned Davis about his investors and his background. On the latter point, they found their pinning predicament. According to the *Chronicle*, when Roberts questioned Davis about his arrest

Charges Fly as Davis Fights for Mat License

Wrestler Suing Promoter Sigel

Fate or Arson?

Davis Fire Is Probed

Credits:

1) Houston Chronicle, July 1, 1949

2) AP version of story, July 20, 1949

3) Houston Post, July 9, 1949

4) Houston Chronicle, Oct. 31, 1948

$350,000 Olympiad Seating 8000 to Be Erected

Home Sales Slump On Local Market

Sports Center Will Also Have Large Club Room

Hugh S. Barlow Plans Four Other Smaller Branch Gymnasiums

record, he denied serving time, or anything since his youth. He admitted to youthful indiscretions in the past, but said he had never been convicted and had not been arrested since his time in California in the 1930s. The record showed Davis had been arrested at least 17 times, had taken a 1935 plea bargain in a robbery case in Houston and served a five-year suspended sentence.

An Associated Press version of the story added more details, calling the hearing unprecedented in Texas Labor history. The story described Davis, 34, as an 18-year veteran of the sport, "wearing a stylish dark-blue sports jacket and chain-smoking king sized cigarettes." Davis stated he planned to sell a quarter of the promotion to Gorgeous George. "If I get the license, I'll bring the best wrestlers in the nation to Texas and not tie them up with any long-term contracts." Lieberman blamed the delay in a decision on Sigel and his 15 or 20 state-wide promoters and the influence they have on the state.

Instead of getting his license, Davis lost nearly everything during the first week of July. According to the *Houston Post* on July 9, 1949, Davis lost his license case Tuesday, July 5. The next day, his neon sign business burned down. Two days later, he and his family woke to find their house on fire. They evacuated safely, but reportedly lost everything, including all of the elaborate robes Davis used. Lieberman requested an arson investigation on behalf of his client. The article put the worth of the uninsured business at $7,500 and the house and possessions at $21,000, but insured for $10,000.

Davis responded with lawsuits. He appealed his verdict, sued Sigel for $110,000 for supposedly controlling the outcome, re-filed after jurisdictional issues, and ultimately got nowhere with his lawsuits and appeals. One response from the Houston office included an all-cap section of a legal filing explaining in detail the perjury committed by Davis during his hearing and a helpful reminder of state perjury laws.

According to wrestling historian Tim Hornbaker, Davis courted the NWA cartel at this time, too. "In separate letters to (Pinky) George, (Al) Haft and (Sam) Muchnick, dated Nov. 3, 1949, Davis wrote: 'Please accept this as a formal request that you recognize me as a member of the National Wrestling Alliance.'" Davis announced that he had "arenas in Houston, seating 7,200, Dallas, seating 3,500, and San Antonio, seating 6,300." He followed up by saying he had 18 years of experience in wrestling and personally invested $20,000 in his current promotional endeavor.

"Four days later, Muchnick returned a letter to Davis in Almeda, Texas, telling him that his application had been received and would be placed on file until the membership could decide. However, Muchnick explained that the NWA was geared more toward promoters with booking offices, and since Davis hadn't yet promoted any matches, plus the fact that there were already NWA-affiliated promoters in his said towns, he wrote, 'I don't know what the decision of the Alliance will be.'"

Muchnick apparently copied his letters to Davis and sent the copies to Sigel, keeping him informed about his rival's movements.

In preparing the book, *Chokehold*, which he co-wrote with football player turned wrestler Jim Wilson, Weldon Johnson made notes from the FBI files on the NWA cartel. J. Michael Kenyon helped him and sent the notes to other historians. They noted Sigel's concern with the opposition group led him to seek NWA membership in 1949.

On March 9, 1950, Sigel sent a wire to Sam Muchnick: "We are proud to be members of the Alliance. Organization is proving behind a doubt it deserves the best from all members as witness splendid stand it has taken on the Texas matter. Long live the Alliance."

Sigel had been the person who brokered peace in St. Louis between Muchnick and star wrestler Lou Thesz when they were in a promotional war. During Sigel's various wars, Muchnick and the NWA supported Sigel by sending Thesz to Texas as much as possible.

Ultimately, Davis did get to stage his wrestling shows. In March 1950, banker Joseph Meyer Jr. formed the Olympiad Sporting Club and contracted with Benbow for use of his arena. Davis not only agreed to headline, but he convinced his neighborhood friend Gorgeous George to main event against him. Or, he almost did.

Sigel took the booking of George seriously and behind the scenes, he used his power and new NWA affiliation to prevent George from appearing, according to the notes by Johnson and Kenyon. Johnny Doyle and Toots Mondt were blamed or given credit for making the booking and Sigel and Muchnick discussed putting pressure on both promoters. "I think we should take steps at the meeting toward straightening out Toots Mondt, Gorgeous George and any other troublemaker," Sigel wrote Muchnick.

Despite being offered a piece of the opposition promotion in Houston, George, via manager Doyle, canceled his appearance. Davis would charge NWA collusion and the hype for the match shifted. Lumberjack McDonald took George's place, but ads continued to reflect a grandstand challenge to George.

Frank Burke, Sigel's brother-in-law and TWA co-owner, sued Davis and another main event wrestler, Juan Humberto, over breach of contract and was counter-sued. The contracts were deemed unenforceable and Meyer's matches were allowed to continue.

Wednesday, March 22, 1950, the Olympiad had its first wrestling show, with about 1,000 fans in attendance, according to the *Chronicle* the next day. Davis won his match in two falls. "The bout was a bloody one, with Davis furnishing the plasma in its rawest form."

Sigel and the Houston establishment countered at the City Aud on Friday, March 24, with their own brawl, as "Wild" Bill Longson beat McShain, billed as for the World's Roughhouse Championship, two falls to one. Ernie Dusek beat Black Guzman and Nell Stewart beat Mae Young on the undercard in a women's match. Hornbaker's research lists the attendance at 3,500.

Two days later, four days after the Olympiad show, the *Post* and journalist Jack Gallagher had a three column, inside page scoop on the wrestling war, complete with pictures of Meyer and Sigel and a headline that read: "Sigel, Meyer Draw Lines For Wrestling War Here."

Section 2 Sunday, March 26, 1950 THE HOUSTON POST Page 3

Sigel, Meyer Draw Lines For Wrestling War Here

By JACK GALLAGHER

Wrestling On Tonight At Olympiad

The Olympiad Sporting Club will stage its first wrestling show at the Olympiad Arena tonight.

Sterling (Dizzy) Davis, former heavyweight champion of Texas, will meet Lumberjack McDonald in the two-out-of-three-fall feature event. Davis is now free to wrestle in Texas after being judged the winner in a temporary injunction suit.

McDonald will be making his first appearance here. He started wrestling in the Northwest lumber camps for the fun of it but turned professional after he had taken the measure of all the "jacks" in the territory.

Two glamour gals, Juanita Coffman and Joan Greene, will tangle in a feature event which promises to be no powder puff affair.

Another new face to make its appearance in the Olympiad tonight will be the Farmer, Waxahachie farmer.

The Farmer will meet Chale Martinez, a roughhouse Mexican boy who knows his way around in the ring.

Gorgeous George, whose manager signed him to a contract to meet Davis tonight, has broken his contract and refused to appear.

Starting time for the show is at 8:30 p.m. Tickets will be on sale until 5 p.m. at Bond's and will be on sale beginning at 7 p.m. at the Olympiad, 2418 Center. A special section has been reserved for negro fans.

Dizzy Davis In Mat Win At Olympiad

Dizzy Davis, an old campaigner in the wrestling business, scored a win Wednesday night at the Olympiad over Lumberjack McDonald.

The main event topped the opening mat venture of Promoter Joseph Meyer. Some 1000 fans were on hand.

Davis took the first fall in 18 minutes with a body press and copped the over-all decision in a hurry in the minute-old second fall when the Lumberjack was disqualified.

McDonald was stubborn in his refusal to break an illegal hold, so Referee Shadow Harmon thumbed him out.

The bout was a bloody one, with Davis furnishing the plasma in its rawest form.

The Farmer employed a head scissors to take a straight fall victory over Chale Martinez in the top prelim. Juanita Coffman won her match when Joan Greene was disqualified, and Juan Humberto, another old-timer in the mat game, used up 12 minutes in pinning Johnny Gallagher.

Sterling (Dizzy) Davis

Lumberjack McDonald

Dizzy Davis will be in the ring waiting for Gorgeous George next Wednesday night at the Olympiad Arena. It's a date Dizzy will keep. Will George?

George was legally signed to a contract by his manager, Johnny Doyle. If George breaks his contract, President Joseph F. Meyer, Jr., of the Olympiad Sporting Club will immediately start proceedings to have George barred from Texas, California and 21 other states.

The Olympiad Sporting Club has promised to give Houston wrestling fans the top stars in the business. We intend to keep that promise.

If George fails to show up, Dizzy Davis will meet Lumberjack McDonald, heavyweight champion of the Northwest.

Sincerely,
Joseph F. Meyer, Jr.

Tickets are on sale at Bond's. The Olympiad Arena is located at 2418 Center, one block north of 2400 Washington.

Credits:
1) Houston Post, March 26, 1950
2) Houston Chronicle, March 22, 1950
3) Houston Chronicle, March 23, 1950
4) Houston Chronicle, March 19, 1950

"Meyer, a social register blue blood who now promotes the spilling of red blood, held his first show Wednesday at the new Olympiad Club."

The story lists the TWA circuit as 19 towns, with 140 wrestlers under contract. The challenge to the contracts and Burke's failed injunction were noted, as was a 1930s challenge to Sigel by Memphis promoter Charley Rentrop. After a section of the article about Meyer's background, he declares Houston big enough for two shows. Later in the story, a one-graph accusation attributed to "one side" claimed the double shows were a plot to kill wrestling and boost boxing in the city again.

"The battle lines have been drawn," the story concludes. "Sigel or Meyer stand to lose a lot of money. Certainly it would seem that both of them cannot prosper if competition continues to be intense. Listen closely the next time you attend a wrestling match. A few of those grunts and groans are authentic and are being emitted back in the box office, where the worried promoters are counting the dwindling receipts."

The second Olympiad show took place Wednesday, March 29, with a rematch between Davis and Lumberjack McDonald that Davis won, plus three other matches, including a women's match. Sigel countered Friday, March 31, and Hornbaker reported 3,700 fans went to see Guzman beat Ernie Dusek, while winning the third fall by disqualification, and McShain and Rito Romero wrestle to a no contest.

Both promotions made big moves in April. Wednesday, April 3, at the Olympiad, Hornbaker reported the attendance at 1,500 as The Farmer beat the Zebra Kid by disqualification in the third fall and Davis drew Humberto in 30 minutes. Red Lyons was also on the card. Friday, April 5, at the City Aud, the attendance held at 3,700, as McShain beat Romero, and Guzman and Carlos Moreno beat Red Berry and Dusek.

A *Post* article March 31, with the headline "Meyer Moves to Import Matmen" detailed a new talent agreement Meyer made with Toots Mondt and new general manager Ray Fabiani. The article, written by Gallagher, did not compliment Meyer's early efforts, calling them "two feeble promotions" but leaving an impression Mondt would be bringing the biggest talent in the world to the Olympiad, which the New York matman praised as "one of the finest in the country, something of which Houston can be proud." Fabiani is quoted saying Houston will see the greats of the business perform, with Argentina Rocca, Jim Londos and Dutch "Nature Boy" Rhodes among the wrestlers mentioned.

An article in the *Post* a week later promised Buddy Rogers would appear on the April 19 show, but instead Londos appeared at Fabiani's Olympiad debut Wednesday, April 19. Both papers upped their coverage and the crowd spiked to 2,600, the best crowd in Meyer's run. Londos beat Lumberjack McDonald in one fall in 24 minutes, beating him so badly the ringside doctor stopped the match. Davis and Lyons went to a no contest in one of the semi-finals when the Zebra Kid attacked Davis before the match to set up a return.

Londos, the Greek star who became an icon in his native land, had been the biggest star in wrestling in the 1920s and 1930s. He was 56 in 1950, but his name still meant something. Fabiani had been promoting shows with him in opposition in Chicago in the early 1950s, as well as several other cities.

"This had to do with working with Faby, who was his business partner on so many occasions," said historian Steven Johnson, who wrote the biography, *Jim Londos, the Golden Greek of Professional Wrestling*. "He was not a member of the NWA and mostly freelanced at that point. I assume he had a cut of Faby's action or maybe even underwrote him. It's in the book that Faby owed him money when Faby went bankrupt in early 1951 and possibly that was related to Chicago, St. Paul or Houston or more places. Never an NWA guy."

In the Olympiad, the return without Londos returned to the normal crowd within two weeks. After the Londos appearance, the promotion lasted just three more shows. April 26, Davis and Ivan Kameroff beat Lyons and Zebra Kid. May 3, bodybuilder Gene Stanlee, billed as wrestling's Mr. America, got a build up for a main event versus Davis. He ended up beating the Zebra Kid in a swerve instead, after Kid knocked Davis out before the match.

Burke Files Lawsuit Against Juan Humberto

Frank J. Burke, brother-in-law of Wrestling Promoter Morris P. Sigel, filed a suit in district court Monday against another of the wrestlers who have contracted to perform at the new Olympiad Arena.

This time the defendant is Juan Humberto who, the petition says, appeared on the Olympiad show March 22 and is booked to wrestle again March 29.

An injunction is asked to restrain Humberto from violating a two-year contract he is claimed to have with Burke not to make any appearances of which Burke does not approve. Humberto's contract, which it is said was a renewal, was dated Jan 28, 1949, and is similar to those Burke has with about 139 other professional wrestlers.

The court action is almost identical with that brought against Wrestler Dizzy Davis recently by Burke. In that case, District Judge Dan W. Jackson required Davis to post a $7500 indemnity bond to protect Burke against any damage Burke may be able to prove because of contract violation when the case is finally tried on its merits.

Burke, who said he would be damaged $30,000 if Humberto continues to breach his contract, asked as an alternative that Humberto be required to post an indemnity bond.

When Attorney John G. Cramer filed the suit Monday, District Judge Ben Moorhead asked if the courts are going to have to hear suits against all of the wrestlers Burke claims to have under contract as booking agent.

Mr Cramer said that would depend on how many threatened to violate their agreements.

Wrestler Files Monopoly Suit Against Burke

A legal fight over a wrestler's contract was carried into federal court Thursday by an attorney who claims federal anti-trust laws have been violated.

A PETITION filed by Bernard Golding, attorney for Wrestler Juan Humberto, alleged that Booking Agent Frank Burke's holding contracts with 139 or 140 wrestlers constitutes a monopoly.

Burke, brother in law of Houston Wrestling Promoter Morris P. Sigel, originally filed an injunction suit against Humberto in state district court.

Burke seeks to prevent Humberto from performing again at Houston's new Olympiad Arena. He also seeks $35,000 in damages alleged to have been suffered when Humberto appeared at the Olympiad March 22.

The case was transferred to federal court after Golding filed an answer to Burke's suit.

Golding contends Humberto did not understand he was signing a contract with Burke. He also claims the contract is invalid, unenforceable and contrary to Texas laws.

Meyer Moves To Import Matmen

JOSEPH MEYER AND RAY FABIANI

Credits:
1) Houston Post, March 28, 1950
2) Houston Post, April 7, 1950
3) Houston Post, March 31, 1950

Davis did not appear on the last Olympiad card, which was May 10. Ivan Kameroff beat Joe Carney and Lumberjack McDonald beat Bill Sledge in the last wrestling matches in the building that season. However, Davis would return to wrestling in Houston quickly. Or, he would return to fighting in Houston, in any event.

With the opposition tasting success, Sigel and his crew countered with a big show Friday, May 5, at the Sam Houston Coliseum, dubbed the Parade of Champions. The earliest Parade of Champions noted so far by wrestling historians is 1939 in Buffalo, but Sigel adopted it for his wrestling war, making every match for a title and headlining with Lou Thesz defending the NWA World title against Bill Longson. Ed "Strangler" Lewis would be the special referee in the NWA match. *Houston Post* columnist Clyde La Motte refereed the Texas women's title match between Nell Stewart and Carol Cook. In the other matches, McShain challenged Guzman for the Texas title, Carlos Moreno and Rito Romero beat Timmy Geohagen and Ruffy Silverstein for the Texas tag titles and Black champion Don Blackman beat Don Kindred.

Built in 1937 as a rodeo hall and convention space, the Coliseum could seat 10,000 for wrestling. Sigel's Gulf Athletic Club would use the Coliseum infrequently for big shows, and made it the full-time venue in 1963, leading to more than two decades of Friday nights at the Coliseum. In the 1980s, it was reconfigured to 12,000-plus seats. In 1971, Houston photo journalist Geoff Winningham put out a wonderful coffee table photo book, *Friday Night in the Coliseum*, which captured the essence of the building and its connection to weekly wrestling. There is also a documentary version available on the internet. A Rice University graduate, Winningham "changed how Texans see themselves," according to *Texas Monthly*.

In 1950, the Parade gamble paid off. The *Post* reported the 10,000-fan crowd to be the biggest in Texas wrestling history and the gate of $15,000 ($204,460 in 2025, according to the inflation calculator) as the biggest in Texas wrestling history. The attendance not only quadrupled the size of the Londos crowd at the Olympiad, but it also nearly tripled the average size of the City Aud crown. Fabiani's work had more than doubled his crowd for one week, but the reality was he was at about 12% capacity in most of his Olympiad shows, and the Londos show raised that to 32.5%. The establishment responded by running its biggest show ever, in a 10,000-seat arena, drawing the largest gate in state history.

May 16, 1950, La Motte delivered the last rites in a section of his *Post* column sub-headlined "Seems Sigel Has Won Again". "It would seem that the effort to supply a wrestling show in opposition to Morris Sigel has fallen on its face. A promotion backed by Joseph Meyer, the banker, has been sponsoring a wrestling show at the Olympiad each Wednesday for several weeks, but there is no show scheduled this week. Mr. Meyer, asked if this were the end, had no comment other than that the Olympiad would be dark this Wednesday. However, Hugh Benbow said he is going to shift the amateur boxing card from Thursday nights to Wednesday nights. And he said he was planning to open the Olympiad to roller skating five nights a week."

In the May 1950 NWA bulletin, Muchnick quoted Sigel: "Sterling (Dizzy) Davis came into our office today (May 12) and admitted he made a bad mistake and was completely and thoroughly licked. They drew $39.66 in Dallas last night. In Houston, Mr. America drew about $400 while we drew more than $14,000 with our card; and Londos drew about $900."

In the same letter, Sigel asked NWA promoters to now show mercy on the wrestlers who worked for the opposition, naming 12 workers. "I wish you would give this mature judgement and please go along with these unfortunates."

Davis returned to the City Aud on Friday, March 19, disturbing the main event between McShain and Moreno. He "cut McShane badly" according to newspaper reports and set up the next several months of wrestling, including two weeks of McShain as a surrogate for Morris Sigel in the ring against Davis. A *Chronicle* article May 24, headlined "Mat Chief Assures Davis He Will Get Fair Deal Friday" continued to pull at the real threads of the feud. "Deputy Commissioner Billy Smith put a stop to all the talk by Dizzy Davis that he might

Dizzy Davis To Meet McShane At City Auditorium

Bitter Mat Rivals to Renew Feud on Sigel's Card Friday.

[illegible]

Davis and McShane Mat Match Friday To Be Grudge Affair

Wrestling Promoter Morris Sigel, who usually watches his Friday night matches from a stage seat at the City Auditorium, is going to move down into the ringside for this week's clash between Dizzy Davis and Irish Danny McShane. The veteran promoter has more interest in Friday's clash than any he has ever promoted, since he and Davis have been feuding for more than a year.

"I didn't want to put Davis in this match or any match," said Sigel. "He has cost me thousands of dollars in legal fees with his lawsuits and hasn't won any of them. I am glad Friday's match is on a winner-take-all basis because I won't have to pay him a penny for his work. Dizzy asked for it and I am sure Danny will give it to him."

Interest in the scrap is mounting among the wrestling fraternity as well as among the fans. Sigel announced that grapplers were heading for Houston from as far as a thousand miles away to see the scrap. World's Champion Louis Thesz has cancelled plans to fly North and will stay to see it. "Wrestlers can smell a grudge match a mile off," said Sigel, "and they wouldn't miss this for anything. Neither would I."

WRESTLING

CITY AUDITORIUM, Friday, June 2nd, 8:30 P.M.

Last week's battle between this pair was the wildest, bloodiest brawl ever seen in any ring. This week promises to be wilder! Don't miss it!

Dizzy

DAVIS

[illegible]

vs.

DANNY

McSHANE

[illegible]

PLUS! A PARADE OF BRAND NEW MAT TALENT AND YOUR POPULAR FAVORITES!

[illegible]

McShane To Meet Davis Again Friday

Irish Danny McShane and Sterling (Dizzy) Davis renew their bloody wrestling rivalry Friday night in the main event of Promoter Morris Sigel's card at the City Auditorium.

McSHANE WAS the winner last Friday in one of the bloodiest bouts ever seen in Houston. Following the match the pair pummeled each other in the ringside seats until police halted the action.

In a tag team match the Zebra Kid and Al (Spider) Galento go against Rito Romero and Carlos Moreno in a one fall to a finish tag team match.

Danny Plechas, a newcomer from the Midwest with an impressive record, tangles with George Pencheff.

Other bouts send Jack Steele against Al Lovelock and Cowboy Carlson against Leo Newman.

Credits:

1) Houston Chronicle, May 21, 1950
2) Houston Chronicle, May 22, 1950
3) Houston Chronicle, May 29, 1950
4) Houston Chronicle, May 28, 1950

not get a square deal when he wrestles Irish Danny McShane at the City Auditorium on Friday night," began the piece without a byline. "I think Davis is away (sic) off base when he suggests that he may not get a fair shake," Smith is quoted as saying. "I was very lenient with him last week when he tried to break up the show. Davis forgets that I don't work for Sigel or any other promoter, I work for the state of Texas, and I am here to see that everyone gets treated right."

Sigel is also quoted: "I agree with Billy. I think Friday's match will be one of the roughest ever seen here, but I don't think Dizzy has to worry about anyone but McShane and I think that's enough worry for any man. There have been a lot of harsh words back and forth but when Dizzy steps in the ring he is on his own and I think McShane will handle him."

The next day's *Chronicle* continued the storyline, again, without noting the writer. "McShane has been humiliated by the way Davis cut and battered him last Friday in an unscheduled set-to that Dizzy brought about to try to force his way back into the local wrestling picture. The match will mark the first meeting between the pair in 15 months and has all the earmarks of being the wildest of a feud that tops all others with local grappling fans. McShane will be out to avenge not only his dislike of Davis, but he will be carrying Promoter Morris Sigel's grudge into the ring with him, too. Sigel has been sued by Davis and has spent a lot of money defending the cases, none of which Dizzy has been able to win." The story concluded by saying Davis would take the Texas title away from Texas if he won.

The *Chronicle* stories ran all week, yet they undersold the feud. The ads gave the promotional spin. "Dizzy Davis, Who says he has been frozen out of Houston Wrestling and promises to blast his way back in by sending the Texas Champion to the hospital! Vs. Danny McShane, Who promises to keep Davis out of the City Auditorium ring for another year by sending him to the hospital in a match that promises to be the bloodiest of their feud!"

The promotion paid off with a reported sell-out crowd of 4,000 fans, according to the *Post* on May 27. McShain won the first fall in 16 minutes with Davis getting the equalizer just 55 seconds later. McShain won the final fall in 20 minutes, despite being thrown into the post and busted open. "McShane then opened a two-fisted attack to the eye and had Davis covered in blood. Dizzy came back, forced McShane into the ropes and ripped open Danny's eye with a series of rights. When (referee Leo) Voss tried to step between the brawlers he ran into a right that dropped him. It was then that McShane dropped Davis and covered for the fall."

The rematch formed immediately for Friday, June 2. "Last week's battle between this pair was the wildest, bloodiest brawl ever seen in any ring. This week promises to be wilder. Don't miss it," read the ad. "Dizzy Davis, Who has lost none of his sock and looks better than ever ... Danny McShane, Who will be out to take Dizzy apart with every trick he knows ..." A *Post* article May 28 added to the hype, mentioning the previous match was only halted by police after McShane and Davis fought into the crowd.

The *Chronicle* ran two more articles, focused around the task of the third man in the ring. The May 30 edition had an unbylined story headlined, "Davis, McShane let off steam on referee choice" and the paper followed up the next day with the cliffhanger, "Boesch accepted by Davis, McShane as mat referee" as announcer Paul Boesch stepped in for Voss. "Naming of Boesch to the post ends a controversy that has been raging between Davis and McShane," the story read. "Last week Referee Leo Voss handled the scrap and is still bruising a cut head and a pair of bruised ribs. Boesch, with plenty of experience as a wrestler and as a referee, was accepted by both men."

According to the *Chronicle* follow-up June 3, it was actually Sarpolis who refereed the bout. Davis won the first fall with his backbreaker to put the Texas title in peril, but McShain won the second fall on a top rope disqualification. After Danny battered Davis in the third fall with fists to the head and knees to the chin, Sarpolis stopped the match because Davis was bleeding from the mouth.

McShain lost the Texas title to Romero in Dallas. The next week in Houston,

WRESTLING
CITY AUDITORIUM
HOUSTON
FRIDAY, MARCH 24
The Wildest Scrap In Years!
WILD BILL
LONGSON
vs.
IRISH DANNY
McSHANE
For the World's Rough House Championship!

ERNIE DUSEK
vs.
BLACK GUZMAN

NELL STEWART
vs.
MAE YOUNG

No Increase in Prices
$1.20, $1.80, $2.40 and $3.00
On Sale Auditorium Hotel Drugstore
Reservations Phone Blacow 2616
Morris Sigel, Promoter

WRESTLING
City Auditorium
Friday, April 14, 8:30 p.m.
Danny Cannot Use the Ring Post!
Rito
ROMERO
vs.
Danny
McSHANE
Two Referees in the Ring!

GUZMAN vs. TERRY
DUSEK vs. PENCHOFF

Tickets: $1.20, $1.80, $2 and $3.
On sale TUESDAY Auditorium Hotel Drugstore. Reservations: BL-2616.
Morris Sigel
Promoter

WRESTLING
Sam Houston Coliseum
Friday, May 5, 8:30 P.M.
THE PARADE OF CHAMPIONS!
The Greatest Wrestling Show Ever HELD in the South!
EVERY BOUT A TITLE BOUT!
WORLD'S HEAVYWEIGHT TITLE
Killer KOWALSKI
vs.
LOUIS THESZ
The champion faces the toughest contender in the game in the 6-ft.-7-inch, 272-pound giant.
2 out of 3 falls, 90 minutes
For the Texas State Title!
Black GUZMAN
vs.
Danny McSHANE
2 out of 3 falls, 90 minutes
One Fall to a Finish
GIRLS' TEXAS TITLE
TEXAS TAG TEAM TITLE
NEGRO WORLD'S TITLE
This Card of Champions Will NOT Be Televised
RESERVED SECTION FOR COLORED
Tickets: $1.80, $2.40, $3.00 and $4.00. On Sale MONDAY
Auditorium Hotel Drugstore
Reservations Phone Blacow 2616
Morris Sigel, Promoter

Mat Card Moves Into Coliseum

Houston's wrestling war becomes warmer this week as Promoter Morris Sigel, who has been operating in the limited seating capacity of the Auditorium, moves his Friday night card to the Sam Houston Coliseum.

SIGEL WILL offer Louis Thesz against 275-pound Killer Kowalski in the main event, with Ed (Strangler) Lewis as the referee.

Kowalski first tossed the Irish strongman, Timmy Geohagen, and then last week put Danny McShane, along with two of his seconds, out of action.

Black Guzman battles McShane in a best two out of three fall clash. Nell Stewart, Texas women's champion, puts her trophy on the line against Carol Cook of Toledo, Ohio.

LOUIS THESZ
Tackles the Killer

tackles Dan Kinkel of New York.

CHAMPIONSHIPS will be on

George To Take On Dizzy Davis

Gorgeous George, the nation's Number 1 wrestling attraction, meets Sterling (Dizzy) Davis in the main event of Promoter Morris Sigel's card at the Auditorium Friday night, with a capacity crowd expected.

GORGEOUS GEORGE
Coming Here

Brenham Host To Tourney

Seems Sigel Has Won Again

It would seem that the effort to supply a wrestling show in opposition to Morris Sigel has fallen on its face.

A promotion backed by Joseph Meyer, the banker, has been sponsoring a wrestling show at the Olympiad each Wednesday for several weeks, but there's no show scheduled this week.

Mr Meyer, asked if this were the end, had no comment other than that the Olympiad would be dark this Wednesday.

However, Hugh Benbow said he is going to shift the amateur boxing card from Thursday nights to Wednesday nights. And he said he was planning to open the Olympiad to roller skating five nights a week.

Benbow has no connection with the wrestling, other than renting the building for it, but apparently doesn't figure the wrestling will continue at the Olympiad.

Credits:
1) Houston Post, March 22, 1950
2) Houston Chronicle, April 10, 1950
3) Houston Post, March 30, 1950
4) Houston Chronicle, April 30, 1950
5) Houston Post, July 9, 1950
6) Houston Post, May 16, 1950

McShain transitioned to a challenge from another Olympiad headliner, the Zebra Kid George Bollas.

Davis went back to the Texas loop and went back to doing business, but the grudge carried forward. So did the payback. In July, Sigel announced another big match. Gorgeous George would return to Houston to take on Davis on Friday, July 14. "Davis already holds one victory over George and sees another triumph as a springboard to national fame," read a *Post* article in the July 9 edition. The *Chronicle* article three days later had more of the real storyline. "Dizzy has been waiting for the Gorgeous One ever since George's alleged run out last spring. ... George's run out rankles heavily with Dizzy since it cost the local boy plenty in cash and prestige."

George hadn't been in Houston in two years, according to the *Post*, and the fans were eager to see the Eastside Houston hero return. Sigel told the *Chronicle* he turned away a record 4,000 fans, while 5,500 fans did get in, and the event drew a reported $7,000 gate ($94,000 in 2025 money). George won the first fall in 12 minutes. Davis used the backbreaker to even the score in seven minutes. In the third fall, Davis missed a charge and flew out of the ring, returning just before the count out, only to receive a series of slams and the final pin.

A Gallagher column in the *Post* on July 30, again summed up the affair, noting Sigel had made $22,000 and run two of his biggest shows ever in the past two months. "Competition has been driven out and wrestling is booming in Houston and all over the state ... all of which brings a smile to Sigel's round face and a bulge in the vicinity of his back pocket, not altogether traced to the barrel which Morris carries around for a waistline." Ever the promoter, Sigel made sure to tell Gallagher that George would return in September, and Thesz would return to defend the world title against Buddy Rogers on Aug. 4.

"Just say that wrestling is in a very healthy condition," Sigel said. "Houston leads the state in attendance; every city in Texas shows an increase in attendance."

"A while back, when the wrestling war was at its height, legal beagle Sigel had more suits pending than Hart, Schaffner and Marx," the column continued.

"Now he reports he has dropped them all. In his beneficence, Sigel even forgave that culprit of the courts, Dizzy Davis."

Tellingly, the column ended with a discussion about the George-Davis show not being televised because George's contract gave him a percentage of the gate. "Now let's see," Sigel pondered. "Which would look best in the paper; to say that we televise every bout except the main event or to say that we televise through the semifinal. Maybe you better just say that we televise through the semifinal."

Titles Go on Line In Wrestling War

Five matches, each for one of the wrestling world's many championships, will be staged Jan. 6 by Promoter Norman Clark, who is moving to Dallas to offer direct competition to Ed McLemore in a battle for wrestling patronage.

Announcement of the card, headed by a duel between Heavyweight Champion Lou Thesz and Mr. Moto, was the first salvo in what may develop into a long and bitter wrestling "war."

Clark represents a Houston syndicate, whose operators formerly were close associates of Promoter McLemore. An argument over the distribution of television receipts led to a parting of the ways between McLemore and the Houston group.

Now, it appears, each side is determined to run the other out of business in Dallas.

The site for Clark's show will be Pappy's Showland. Karl Sarpolis, matchmaker for McLemore for many years, will now handle the same job for Clark.

McLemore has said he will continue to stage matches each Tuesday night at the Sportatorium. The rival group will hold its matches on the same night, at Pappy's Showland. Clark said, however, that there would be no show Jan. 13, because the night spot was committed to another attraction.

McLemore also will have a Thursday night program at the Sportatorium.

Besides the Thesz-Moto bout, which will be refereed by Leo Voss, Clark announced these matches for his first show:

Cyclone Anaya will defend his Texas championship against Chief Kit Fox.

Woody Strode, Negro titlist, will meet Tex Grady of Chicago.

Nell Stewart, Texas women's champion, will wrestle Ethel Brown.

Ray Gunkel and Ricki Star will defend their state tag-team title against Wild Red Berry and Ted Christy.

Credits:
1) Dallas Morning News, Dec. 28, 1952
2) Dallas Morning News, Jan. 4, 1953
3) Dallas Morning News, Jan. 2, 1953

Beck to Join In Mat Derby

The newest entry in Dallas' complicated wrestling competition put in an appearance Saturday with the announcement of a mat card, promoted by Maurice Beck, at the Sportatorium Thursday night.

Headlining the five-bout card will be a match between two grapplers well known in Dallas, Roy Graham and Jack Kennedy.

Mara Duba and Jack O'Brien, both of whom will appear on Tuesday night's Sportatorium card, will meet in the semiwindup, while Johnny Dobbs of Omaha, Neb., and Bob Gurley of Dallas will tangle in a third bout.

Two more preliminaries are being arranged.

WFAA-TV, Channel 8, will telecast all of the card except the main event, beginning at 8:30 p.m.

6-Event Mat Card Slated

Ed McLemore, wrestling promoter here for the last fourteen years, Wednesday announced a double main event card for the opening of the 1953 wrestling season at the Sportatorium next Tuesday night.

Gorgeous George Grant of Hollywood, making his first start in Dallas, will tackle a Dallasite, Tommy (Nature Boy) Phelps, who had to leave town to make good in the wrestling wars, in one of the two-out-of-three-falls cofeatures.

Roy Dunn, 230-pounder from Alva, Okla., who claims that he holds five victories over Lou Thesz and that he will bring a heavyweight championship belt here he won from Everett Marshall, will face rough-grappling Jack Bernard, another newcomer to Dallas, in the other coheadliner.

Billy Sandow, who managed Ed (Strangler) Lewis and Marshall when they were heavyweight champions, recently came out of retirement to serve as Dunn's manager and will be here for the match.

McLemore said that four other bouts would be presented on the first 1953 mat card.

Changing his first-announced program, the veteran Dallas grappling promoter said that a grappler who bills himself as Elephant Boy will face newcomer Ken O'Connor of Indianapolis in the semiwindup.

A team match will send a popular Dallas Irishman, Jack Kennedy, and his young protege, Gene Allbert of Denton, against veterans Roy Graham and Jack O'Brien. Two more newcomers, Johnny Dobbs, ex-cowboy from Omaha, Neb., and Mara Duba of South America, will tangle. Leo (The Lion) Newman also will appear on the card, but his opponent has not been announced.

4

Staging

Houston Wrestling closed 1952 with a big show and its annual plan to hype an even bigger show for the beginning of the new year. Morris Sigel and company traditionally ran 50 weeks a year, and so December hype focused on the Christmas party and show, usually the third Friday of the month, and the new year show. The prevailing belief was a two-week layoff made routine fandom harder and great emphasis fell on enticing the fans back for a January super show.

The 1952 season closed Dec. 19, with the annual benefit for the *Chronicle*'s The Goodfellow Fund to provide toys to needy kids, ages two to 10. The Dec. 20 edition of the paper called it a crowd-pleasing event. Cyclone Anaya won the Texas title, beating Duke Keomuka, and in the finale, Anaya, Ricki Starr and Ray Gunkel beat Keomuka, Red Berry and Kinji Shibuya. Dizzy Davis also wrestled, beating Jack O'Reilly by disqualification. The paper did not put a number on the crowd but called it a sell out.

Christmas Eve, the *Chronicle* reported a large number of other wrestling promoters would attend the matches Jan. 2. Lou Thesz would defend his NWA World Title against Killer Kowalski, and "Sam Muchnick of St. Louis, Fred Kohler of Chicago, Johnny Doyle of Los Angeles and Pedro Martinez of New York" would be in the audience.

In Corpus Christi the night before, the season closed with a tag team battle as Keomuka and Ike Eakins faced Andre Drapp and "Count" Billy Varga.

In San Antonio, things went back to normal for the season finale Wednesday,

Dec. 17, with Gory Guerrero defeating Drapp, two falls to one, in the main event. The TV guide lists the Wednesday night television on Channel 4 KOAI as 8 p.m. Wrestling Profile and 8:20 Live Wrestling. At 9:30, Hollywood Hits came on the air, leaving San Antonio airwaves main event free. Incidentally, a San Antonio fan could also watch wrestling Monday from Chicago and Saturday from Hollywood, which listed matches that week of George Becker vs. vs. Rito Romero and Bobby Managoff vs. Ted Christy.

Although the paper ran wire stories on the wrestling war looming, the *San Antonio Light* match report that week said nothing about the previous week's issues. It is not confirmed if the return to television took place Dec. 17, as listed, or in 1953. The paper did note the Wrestlethon would be dark on Christmas Eve and New Year's Eve. As with Houston, San Antonio promoted a big first show of 1953. In an article in the *Light* on Dec. 31, matchmaker Frank Brown announced Thesz vs. Anaya for the title as the main event Wednesday, Jan. 7.

In Dallas, there were no matches Tuesday, Dec. 16. What started in San Antonio led Dallas promoter Ed McLemore to decide the Dec. 9 show would wrap up his season. McLemore's words to Pfefer may or may not have been true. Doyle and Sigel may not have had a plan to take over the business with television. However, with the TWA partners and the wrestlers eyeing the Texas Rasslin' money, McLemore weighed his options and decided to book other talent for his shows. He began making plans for Tuesday, Jan. 6.

In the NWA bulletin, President Sam Muchnick said he went to Texas to try to resolve the dispute, without success. "Knowing the story the way I do, as I returned from Texas last Wednesday, I feel that the Houston office is right in its battle with Ed McLemore of Dallas," he wrote. "What the Houston office has done is not detrimental to any member of this group because they are fighting for the rights. ... In my trip to Texas last week I heard more about television of wrestling and filming of wrestling matches than actual wrestling. Sometimes I feel that we should change the name of our organization to the National Wrestling Television Alliance."

McLemore and promoter Jack Pfefer's shared a protege named Tommy "Izzy Becker" Phelps, also known as one of Pfefer's Nature Boys. Phelps arrived back home in Dallas at the end of 1952 to care for his ailing mom and return to the Dallas office where he got his start. He summed up the situation for Pfefer upon arrival in a Dec. 26 letter. "Well, Jack, I called Mr. McLemore and Mr. Beck to say hello but they both are out of the city right now, they told me they were due back in town Saturday or Sunday so I'll give my regards to them from you as soon as I talk to them. I did find out one thing from the boy who works in the office for Mr. McLemore; he said Ed closed down a week earlier than he was going to on account of the television trouble they are having but I couldn't get any more details on it."

A story "Wrestling War Denied By Sigel" in the *Chronicle* on Dec. 27, quoted Sigel as saying "phooey" to the idea of a wrestling war. "We own two-thirds of the Dallas Wrestling Club stock. Now Ed McLemore says he is kicking us out. He owns one third. He also complains that we are going to run in competition against him. May I say that he is going to run in competition to us, and that's all there is to it."

The article then references Sigel's health issues in February, originally reported as a stroke. "Sigel says that the whole thing started when he suffered a heart attack in February and went to a hospital here for a long stay. 'McLemore figured I was through and he decided to take over.'" Sigel alleged McLemore began withholding money from his partners in June. The story concluded by saying the "Texas Wrestling Club" promoters were looking for a Dallas venue to run Tuesdays, the same night as McLemore's Sportatorium shows. Sigel said the wrestlers were under contract and would appear for his promotion when they made their Dallas debut.

Sigel's health issues, and the failed spring attempt by McLemore and Sarpolis to move the booking office to Dallas, weren't the only big news moments of 1952. In the summer, a bombshell dropped on McLemore, too. The July 11 edition of the *Dallas Morning News* reported District Judge Sarah T. Hughes ruled the day before that a quarter of his building was on land owned by the City County Levee Improvement District and the Dallas County Flood Control District. "And the Sportatorium, not the flood control people, will have to move along, the judge ruled — at least, that portion which rests on the wrong side of the old Trinity River channel 'meander' line." The article noted the two state organizations have been taking action against a number of property owners who have expanded into the dried river bed. It noted this action at the Sportatorium was filed against the land owners, William Bond Cox and W.T. Cox, representing the minor Jane Ellen Cox; and the building operator, the Cadiz Corp., which in turn was owned by McLemore. No resolution was announced.

It couldn't have been concern No. 1 in Dallas, where McLemore had decided to leave the TWA and promote his own shows. Despite Sigel's denials, McLemore's plans were in the papers the same week.

In an Associated Press story bylined from Dallas, McLemore indicated he was going to court over wrestler contracts, believing he had the rights for the Texas wrestlers to appear at the Sportatorium and on his television shows. Still, he admitted he was going to bring in a new group of performers, which would put him at a disadvantage.

"McLemore said the struggle may spread over the entire state, and threatened to go to court if necessary with the charge that the Houston agency is conspiring in bring(ing) about a violation of contracts the Dallas promoter says he has with wrestlers furnished by the agency." The article went on to mention McLemore would add a Thursday show.

It quoted Frank Burke as saying the Houston office would also run Tuesdays, at a location to be announced. Pappy's Showland was speculated but not announced as the location, a forecast that turned out true. C.A. "Pappy" Dolsen ran a burlesque nightclub at 500 W. Commerce St. in the Oak Cliff neighborhood, west of downtown Dallas. It opened in 1946 and Dolsen always seemed interested in having wrestling in his club. For a few months in 1950, Pappy's ran shows for the outlaw group led by Dizzy Davis, in an effort to give that group a circuit of their own.

The article concluded with a war of words about the legal affairs. "Burke was quoted by the *News* as saying McLemore 'kicked us out,' contending the Houston office owned two-thirds of the promotion here. McLemore countered: 'If they own two-thirds of it wouldn't they have the controlling interest?'"

Both sides prepped for the first week of January. Tuesday, Jan. 6, would be a head-to-head showdown, with shows at the two venues, which were less than two miles apart. In addition, Beck would run Thursday, Jan. 8.

A Jan. 4, AP story expanded on everyone's plans. McLemore had kept Dallas area wrestlers Jack Kennedy and Roy Graham (also, Jack O'Brien, who was not mentioned) but otherwise was losing access to, "the 'name' wrestlers — grapplers who, over the 15 years McLemore has been promoter supreme in Dallas, have helped build the sport into a $225,000 annual business."

"I know I will have to build them up and that I'll be losing money in the meantime," McLemore said, "but I am not about to move from Dallas. This is an all-out fight."

The story noted the first legal aspect of the case as TWA promoter Norman Clark got a restraining order against McLemore preventing "bodily injury" or

POSTAL RECEIPTS, BUILDING ZOOM

Last 24 Hours in Dallas

[illegible]

OUR POSTAL receipts last year put Baltimore's and Pittsburgh's in the shade, but this may not be something to brag about. A mess of that mail doubtless was duns.

STILL, some people had more money in the bank than ever before. Oddly enough.

VITAMIN VARNELL was in town from Sewanee, Tenn., claiming he was a busy man. Probably never had to get out a lively Monday morning paper on a dull Sunday afternoon.

A LOT OF PERMITS to build things got taken out around here last year, but New York, Los Angeles, Chicago and Detroit beat Dallas. Just a poor fifth, that's us.

LOOKED AS IF Uncle Sam was doing fully a third of his Texas shopping in Big D. Makes sense.

AND WEST DALLAS people were offering prayers of thanksgiving for annexation. One of our senior observers reported little brown eyes wide in wonder at the sight of graders and garbage trucks.

JUDGE KING told the county grand jury, sure, it could stay on and finish what it started: An investigation, apparently, of Commissioners' road and bridge business.

A WRESTLING promoter said he feared bodily harm from another wrestling promoter. Judge Mac Taylor acted as referee. Ordered the feared fellow into a neutral corner.

DETECTIVES had seven men, three women in the pokey. Aimed to clear up a slew of those recent robberies.

AND DOWN in the First Methodist basement, a former pastor of the church was heaped with praise at a dinner attended by [illegible] people. The honoree was Bishop William C. Martin, now the ranking Protestant clergyman of the land. —LORRIE BROOKS

with the tampering of Clark's television transmission. McLemore said he had not been served and mocked the idea. "Gosh, I am a bad, bad boy," he said.

The story said McLemore's talent would come from Billy Sandow, and include world title claimant Roy Dunn. The TWA group would counter with Lou Thesz vs. Mr. Moto at Pappy's. All three shows were scheduled to air that week, Clark's on WFAA Channel 8, and McLemore's Tuesday and new Thursday show on KRLD Channel 4.

On the day of the first head-to-head, the *Morning News* ran an article along with full cards for both shows. "The local wrestling war begins in earnest Tuesday night, with two heavyweight championship claimants appearing on separate programs." The piece noted the court case had been delayed a week because McLemore had still not been served, and he again lambasted the idea he was a threat to Clark. The article noted NWA President Sam Muchnick had been in Dallas on Monday "as an interested spectator" and representing 38 NWA offices, including Sigel's Houston and TWA businesses.

A solid chunk of the story, and the early war promotions in general, focused on the world title claims of Thesz and Dunn, who had largely avoided each other. Dunn, the anti-establishment champ, claimed to be undefeated for the past six years and traced his title to a 1947 win over Everett Marshall. He also boasted of a win over Thesz in Wichita, Kansas. Sandow, his promoter, called Thesz a "synthetic champion" and pointed to the NWA awarding Thesz the title after Orville Brown's car accident as a fictional title win. Muchnick rebutted by saying the NWA only recognized Thesz and defended the legitimacy of his reign.

At Pappy's, the Thesz match was supported by a Parade of Champions-like undercard. Nell Stewart defended the Texas Women's Championship against Ethel Brown. Woody Strode defended the Black Championship against Tex Grady. Ricki Starr and Ray Gunkel defended the Texas Tag Titles against Red Berry and Ted Christy and Cyclone Anaya defended the Texas Title against Chief Kit Fox.

At the Sportatorium, Dunn defended his crown against Jack Bernard. In the co-main event, "Nature Boy" Tommy Phelps wrestled "Gorgeous" George Grant. Elephant Boy (Tony Olivas) vs. Ken O'Connor, Jack Kennedy and Gene Allbert vs. Roy Graham and Jack O'Brien, Johnny Dobbs vs. Mara Duba and Bad Boy Brown vs. Billy Willis rounded out the card.

With a loaded lineup on the TWA show and the familiar setting of the Sportatorium hosting the other show, it set up a test of loyalties. If the fans had abandoned the established venue, it could have ended the war immediately. Instead, the result set the scene for 18 months of battle.

Phelps summed it up to Pfefer in a Dec. 30 letter. "Well, they are having a real war here in Texas and they are going to have live shows here Jan. 6. Morris Sigel and his bunch are running a show at Pappy's Showland and they have a hell of a card lined up Lou Thesz vs. Mr. Moto and they have big posters up all over town. This sure would be a great time to move in and help your great friend Ed McLemore as I imagine he needs a little help now."

RASSLIN'

Dallas Style

10¢

JUNE 30
1953

MR. AMERICA

LIVE STOCK PAVILION
FAIR PARK

ED McLEMORE....Promoter

See America's Most Exciting
WRESTLING MATCHES
on Channel 4
KRLD-TV

KRLD and KRLD T-V

Down at Ringside . . .

ED McLEMORE

Credits:
1) Dallas Rasslin' program from Fair Park, June 30, 1953, including Mr. America Gene Stanlee on cover, with an ad for the television show and feature on Ed McLemore inside, Greg Klein Collection

5
The War Begins

In an undated letter to Jack Pfefer, clearly written in the afterglow of Jan. 6, 1953, Ed McLemore did not waste time with small talk. "Dear Jack," he wrote. "We skunked them the first night — we did 2658, they did 837. Had a pretty good show — am sending you more publicity right away — Thanks for leaving Tommy with me — Will take good care of him. Regards, Ed."

In the battle of familiar wrestlers versus familiar venue, the Sportatorium won. Wrestling fans being creatures of habit no doubt paid off. Still, the Sportatorium sat 6,400, and the win foretold of a protracted battle.

McLemore also had his former wrestlers served with restraining orders from appearing on television in opposition to his shows. The Jan. 7 edition of the *Dallas Morning News* covered Deputy Sheriff Bobby Bass giving out the restraining orders from the 101st District Court 15 minutes before showtime at Pappy's. "But the legal papers failed to stop the TV cameras as five wrestlers and referee Leo Voss defied the orders. Besides Voss, they were Ricki Starr, Cyclone Anaya, Chief Kit Fox, Ralph (Wild Red) Berry and Ray Gunkel. Most of the wrestlers refused to admit their identity as Bass sought out those for whom he had the orders. Many of the papers were strewn about the floor in the crowded makeshift dressing rooms. Gunkel jumped back as Bass approached him with his paper. 'I'm John Jones,' he roared, 'one of the Jones boys.' 'I know you, Ray,' laughed Bass. 'I've seen you wrestle many times.' 'I'm not served,' countered Gunkel. 'I didn't acknowledge my name.'"

When Lou Thesz arrived, he refused his order, too, although his main event was never scheduled to be televised. Matchmaker Doc Sarpolis talked Thesz into taking the papers for publicity. "Sarpolis pleaded with Bass to serve the order in the ring. 'I want the people of Dallas to know that someone's trying to stop them from being televised,' he said. The matches proceeded without any incident. There had been rumors of threats of bodily harm to Norman Clark, promoter of the new wrestling faction. Clark's attorneys last week secured a restraining order against McLemore in the conduct of advertised wrestling matches under Clark's promotion."

The *Morning News* covered the trial the next day, complete with a headline "McLemore loses fall to Clark" and pictures of the wrestlers on the stand: "District Judge Sarah T. Hughes ordered McLemore to stop interfering with Clark's staging and televising of his own wrestling cards in competition with McLemore." Clark said in the article he had a 26-week lease on Pappy's and would go forward with that season of events beginning Jan. 20, as the club had a previous booking the 13th. The piece had photos of Moto and Fox on the stand. It was appropriate "art" as the larger-than-life boys commanded the room and performed for the judge and courtroom audience alike. "But the wrestlers themselves, including World Heavyweight Champion Lou Thesz stole the show in the Fourteenth District court hearing. Several of them testified and all sat attentively in the courtroom during the hearing. Spectators, including many women, crowded into the courtroom for a glimpse of the well-televised and powerfully built wrestlers. Besides Thesz, there were Ricki Starr, Mr. Moto, Cyclone Anaya, Kit Fox, Ralph (Wild Red) Berry and Ray Gunkel."

McLemore claimed he was paying the boys $5 extra per TV broadcast but the wrestlers denied receiving TV pay. "Wild Red Berry, as talkative on the witness stand as he is active in the ring, summed it up. 'They always rush you down to sign just before the match ... I start to read it (the contract) and they say, 'You haven't got time to read this now, just sign it' and I sign it.'"

The article also mentioned the wrestlers defying the previous day's court order from the 101st District Court. McLemore's attorneys said they would

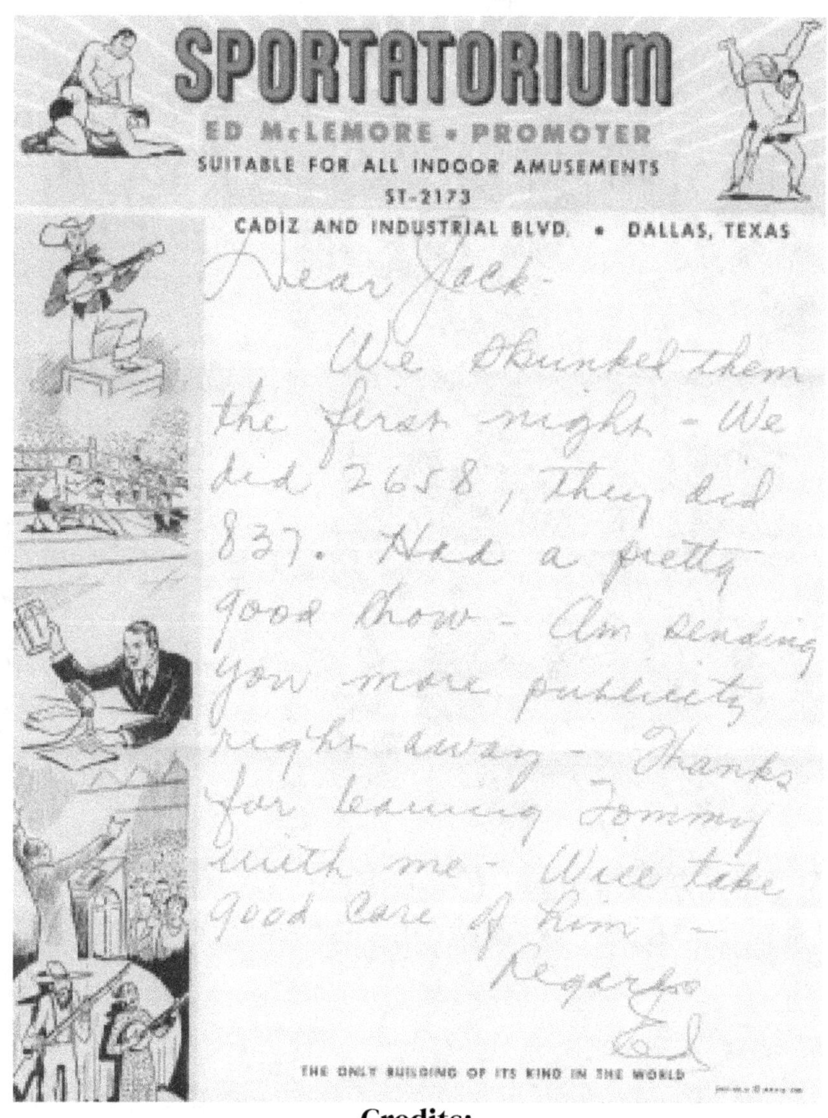

SPORTATORIUM
ED McLEMORE • PROMOTER
SUITABLE FOR ALL INDOOR AMUSEMENTS
ST-2173
CADIZ AND INDUSTRIAL BLVD. • DALLAS, TEXAS

Dear Jack-

We skunked them the first night - We did 2658, they did 837. Had a pretty good show - Am sending you more publicity right away - Thanks for leaving Tommy with me - Will take good care of him -

Regards
Ed

THE ONLY BUILDING OF ITS KIND IN THE WORLD

Credits:

1) Jan. 6, 1953, letter from Ed McLemore to Jack Pfefer. Courtesy of the Rare Books and Special Collections Department, Hesburgh Libraries, University of Notre Dame

Profits of the wrestling program at Peppy's Showland Tuesday night will go to the March of Dimes, to benefit such polio-stricken youngsters as four-year-old Trudy Jo Howell. Trudy Jo is sitting on Chief Kit Fox's knee. Next to Fox is Alo Leiland. In the back are, left, Jeffries, the valet of Gorgeous George, and Al Costello, who will wrestle George in the main event. Leiland and Kit Fox also are on the card. The March of Dimes will benefit from another Tuesday night wrestling show, too—the program to be staged at the Sportatorium.

Gorgeous George, Costello In Main Bout at Showland

Gorgeous George and Al Costello, winner of last week's elimination tournament, will headline Promoter Norman Clark's March of Dimes benefit wrestling card at Peppy's Showland, Tuesday night. Clark will donate the profits to the polio fund. Fans are asked to send contributions to Clark at the White Plaza Hotel.

Clark also has promised that the grapplers will entertain, during intermissions, with songs and special numbers.

George and Costello, former [illegible] champion, will battle two of three falls, with a 30-minute time limit. Five other bouts are scheduled.

A one-fall, 10-minute-limit Negro bout pitting Wilson Moton of California and Emerson Crosier of Dallas will open the card at 8:30 p.m.

In the 30-minute semifinal, Alo Leiland will tackle Mr. Moto in a battle of judo chops.

The preliminaries feature Ricki Starr against Dory Funk and Cyclone Anaya against Jackie Nichols.

Howard (The Hangman) Cantonwine will return after a long absence to meet Chief Kit Fox.

AT SPORTATORIUM

Beck Opens Mat Card Tonight

Following close on the heels of Tuesday night's double-barreled offerings, Promoter Maurice Beck will re-enter the mat picture, after a two-year layoff, with a five-bout card at the Sportatorium Thursday night. The opening match is scheduled for 8:30 p.m.

WFAA-TV, Channel 8, will telecast the first four matches.

Headlining the card will be a 2-of-3-falls feature between Irish Jack Kennedy of Dallas and Roy Graham of Corsicana. Both have appeared here many times.

Bald but bearded Jack O'Brien will tackle South American Mars Duba in the one-fall semifinal.

Other one-fall bouts pit Bob Gurley and Johnny Dobbs, Neal Farmer and Jack Adkisson and a pair of Negro matmen, Wilson Moton and Willie Love.

Credits:

1) Dallas Morning News, Jan. 7, 1953

2) Dallas Morning News, Jan. 8, 1953

likely not pursue the matter.

The story ended with a tale about Thesz feeling like he had not gotten his promised percentage from McLemore and Sarpolis. Thesz indicated he was told it would be made up the next date. Under cross examination, McLemore's attorney asked him if it was made up on the next date. "'We rectified it that night,' Thesz replied, flexing shoulders almost as wide as the judge's bench."

Thursday, Jan. 8, wrestling returned to the Sportatorium for what the paper called Maurice Beck's first show in two years. The main event featured local holdovers "Irish" Jack Kennedy and Roy Graham, while Jack O'Brien faced Mara Duba in the semi-final. Kennedy won to set up a title match with Dunn on the show Tuesday, Jan. 13, where McLemore had the stage to himself again momentarily. Trying to take advantage, McLemore called the card "get acquainted night" and offered buy one get one free tickets.

The Thesz vs. Dunn challenges overshadowed the hometown title shot for Kennedy, with an article in the *Morning News* on Jan. 7. "Night Club Owner Proposes Thesz vs. Dunn Title Bout" introduced Sky Club owner Joe Bonds to the story briefly. Bonds offered his club as a neutral site for the proposed world title showdown between Thesz and Dunn. Bonds said both Clark and McLemore had expressed interest in his idea.

Of course, neither was focused on a third-party solution. Both were still in the staging stage of the war. A Sunday article focused on Clark's new schedule, again highlighting the Jan. 20 return, which would feature a tournament for the right to face Gorgeous George on Jan. 27.

Phelps, a Dallas kid who had been an office boy turned main event star for Pfefer on the recommendation of McLemore, kept Pfefer informed: "Norman Clark is having 13 matches on Tuesday night and George Wagner is supposed to be here Jan. 27 but weather (sic) he will be here or not, I don't know. Maybe you do." As Nature Boy Tommy Phelps, he was using his real name, but in his letters, more often than not, he signs, "as always, your boy, Izzy," based on his earlier gimmick, Izzy Becker.

The attendance the second week at the Sportatorium was lower, Phelps reported Jan. 16. "Well, the house in Dallas was down Tuesday. The boys only got $40 or so they said. There was a good crowd but mostly the people there were free passes. They have been passing out plenty of passes to get the crowd in the arena." Phelps closed by relaying an important message to Pfefer. "McLemore said he really hopes you can help him out in this fight."

The response to wrestling on a new night was underwhelming, too. Phelps wrote to Pfefer on Jan. 18, three days after the second Thursday show: "Well, I worked Dallas on Thursday night and got $25. There wasn't anybody there. They said 450 and that is just about what they had there."

In a letter Jan. 24, Phelps said he made $25 for working Jack Kennedy on the show Jan. 22. Pfefer outlined in red pen: "We worked a finish in the third fall where we were both counted out. It was hot." More importantly, Phelps relayed the story of Happy Humphrey, who worked Jan. 20 at the Sportatorium in the semifinal against Jack Bernard. "Well, Big Humphrey wired Mr McLemore after he left Dallas last Tuesday night and told him he wouldn't be back as he didn't want to work against Sigel and Sarpolis, but I guess you know all about it by now."

Tuesday, Jan. 27 turned into charity night, with dueling shows for the March of Dimes. At the Sportatorium, Kennedy and Johnny Dobbs were advertised in a feud settler, champion Roy Dunn promised to beat two men in 45 minutes or forfeit his purse, with 6-foot-8 Sky High Ross and Silent George Huber both in the ring with Dunn at the same time. Phelps and Elephant Boy against Jack O'Brien and Bill Dusin held the semifinal spot. The show was advertised as McLemore's 14th anniversary show, and fifth with the March of Dimes. The *Morning News* noted the 1952 show raised $11,500 for the charity. At Pappy's, George faced tournament winner Al Costello. Alo Leilani and Mr. Moto had a judo chop match in the semifinal, with Ricki Starr vs. Dory Funk Sr., Cyclone Negro vs. Jackie Nichols, Howard "The Hangman" Cantonwine vs. Chief Kit Fox and Wilson Moton vs. Emerson Crozier rounding out the card.

WRESTLING PROMOTER MAKES $1,000 CHALLENGE

Wants truth to Answer of who is real champion

The question "Who is the real World's Heavyweight Champion?" has been asked many times of Ed McLemore, Dallas wrestling promoter. Just as often, says McLemore, the fans want to know why he doesn't match Roy Dunn vs. Lou Thesz for a world's heavyweight title bout. For those who are not familiar with the facts, Roy Dunn defeated Everett Marshall for the championship and the only recognized title belt in a championship match in Wichita, Kan., on Nov. 1, 1949. Since that time, he has defeated all worthy challengers. Among his victims, is Lou Thesz, one of the present-day crop of title claimants. Thesz is associated with a St. Louis wrestling group which has refused to employ Roy Dunn's services because Dunn won't take orders. Thesz meets only Alliance stooges, many of whom he has beaten many times. The National Wrestling Alliance is a self-serving organization who named Thesz champion behind closed doors in a meeting in September of 1949. Dunn won his title in the ring.

This Tuesday, McLemore's opposition has announced a Texas Heavyweight Championship bout between Ray Gunkel, alleged Texas Heavyweight Title Holder, and Duke Keomuka. Promoter Ed McLemore announces that he will give $1,000 in cash to anyone able to get the synthetic champion, Lou Thesz, and the winner of the Texas Heavyweight Championship bout Tuesday night, to meet Roy Dunn. Dunn agrees to beat both alleged champions in the same night and to donate his share of the purse that night to any reputable charity.

MAT FANS! DON'T BE FOOLED AGAIN!

$1,000 STAKE

McLemore Issues Defy To Thesz Duo

Some spice was added to the local wrestling war Thursday when Promoter Ed McLemore offered $1,000 to anyone who could arrange a match between Roy Dunn and two wrestlers of the opposing camp, Lou Thesz and the winner of the Ray Gunkel-Duke Keomuka scrap next Tuesday night.

McLemore claims that Dunn is the world's heavyweight champion. A similar claim on behalf of Thesz is made by Promoter Norman Clark. Clark is promoting the Gunkel-Keomuka match at Pappy's Showland Tuesday night, which is billed as a state heavyweight title affair.

Dunn will beat the winner of that match, and Thesz, on the following Tuesday night, if such a bout can be arranged, McLemore said.

"Dunn offers to beat both of them the same night," McLemore said, "and he will give his proceeds to charity. The match can be staged at either my place, the Sportatorium, or at Pappy's Showland."

Credits:
1) Dallas Rasslin' ad that ran in programs and newspapers in April 1953
2) Dallas Morning News, April 17, 1953

Phelps reported another win for the Sportatorium crew, but the numbers were trending in the wrong direction: "Well, Tony and I was in a wild tag match last night. We worked an angle I had Jack O'Brien in a full nelson and he ducked and Tony punched me and Tony and I went to it. I used the blade and it really poured. The people were going crazy. So, they have he and I booked next week here in Dallas. It should help draw something anyway. Well, we got $40 and the house wasn't too good. They said we had 1,700 people and that Pappy's Showland had 1,300 people with George on top with Al Costello."

Phelps had no regard for the main event on his show. "Well, I have been in and have seen some stinking matches in my short career in the business but that main event last night between Roy Dunn and his two opponents was the worst I've ever seen in my life. The people were leaving five minutes after it started. He beat Sky High Ross first and then went through with Silent Hubert. Boy, I'm telling you, I can still smell it, it stunk so bad."

The last show of the first month of the war took place Thursday, Jan. 29, at the Sportatorium, with Phelps beating Kennedy in two out of three falls in the main event. Young Jack Adkisson, billed under his real name, beat Al Foreman in the second match. The future Fritz von Erich had debuted for the Dallas group Jan. 8, under the eye of his mentors "Mr. Mac and Mr. Beck," but this was his first hometown win. Soon, as documented in the Pfefer Collection, "Mr. Mac" and "Izzy" were writing letters to Pfefer to get Jack out of town for some seasoning and, perhaps, less exposure during the war. Pfefer did what Pfefer did, he turned Jack ethnic, and the rest is wrestling history told best elsewhere already. However, there is an interesting postscript about Fritz Von Erich and the history of Texas Wrestling that has nothing to do with his boys, but everything to do with the Iron Claw.

As February began, the *Dallas Morning News* announced the war had left the courts. McLemore withdrew his lawsuit and Clark's lawyers claimed victory, according to the article.

At Pappy's on Tuesday, Feb. 3, Clark staged another loaded show, with Alo

Leilani vs. Mr. Moto with stipulations in the main event, plus Chief Kit Fox and Ricki Starr against Dory Funk Sr. and Leo Newman, Big Humphrey vs. Ted Christy, Bull Curry against Billy Varga and Al Costello vs. Cyclone Anaya. Ray Gunkel, a two-time All-American wrestler at Purdue, who also won two AAU National titles as a heavyweight, refereed the main event, Moto's second was barred. At the Sportatorium, Chief Lone Eagle fought Johnny Dobbs, while Phelps took on Elephant Boy (Tony Olivas). Thursday, Feb. 5, Phelps beat Kennedy, Eagle beat Simmons and Elephant Boy beat Mara Duba. In a letter on Feb. 4, Phelps said he made $40 while the Clark show was back down, to 804 fans. "Our crowd last night was bigger than last week and their crowd was smaller than last week," he said.

The next day, Phelps wrote Pfefer again with unusual news: "Well, Paul Boesch (announcer and office man for Morris Sigel's opposition) was at our matches Tuesday night. He came in with Al Costello and sat down and watched a couple of the matches and then left. I think he bought a ticket to come in, also Costello. They just sat there quietly and talked and then got up and walked out."

Phelps noted an offer from Pfefer to leave Dallas and thanked him. It seemed he was aware, business-wise, he should leave, but his concerns for his mother's ill health kept him home. Almost every update on the wrestling war was accompanied with an update on his mom. For instance, on Jan. 28: "Well, Jack, I will close now as I have to go see my mother at the hospital. She is holding her own but that's all. They are trying to get her stronger so they can operate on the liver condition she had, but they are not having much success right now."

Phelps left the business as a 30-something to become an early version of a televangelist in the 1960s, and his affinity for Pfefer seemed to be paired with a growing distaste for the rest of the business. "Thank you for saying I am welcome to come back as soon as my mom is well. That's really nice of you to say that as I have always enjoyed working for you and you have always treated me fair and square and in this rotten filthy business it's not often you find a man who will do right by you like you have by me. They usually stick it in your ass the first

show there Jan 5th well
they are having a real
War here in Texas and
they are going to have
two Shows here Jan 6th
Morris Siegel and his bunch
are running a Show at
Pappy's Showland and they
have a hell of a Card lined
up Lou Thesz and Mr Motto
on top and they have big
posters all over town.
This sure would be a great
time for you to move
in and help your good
Friend Ed McLemore as I
imagine he needs a little
help now. well Ed hasn't

Credits:

1) Dec. 30, 1952, letter from Tommy Phelps to Jack Pfefer. Courtesy of the Rare Books and Special Collections Department, Hesburgh Libraries, University of Notre Dame

chance they get but as I said before you have always been 100 percent with me and I can't forget that."

If Phelps had plans to leave, they were dashed as his mom's health took a turn for the worse. Feb. 11, he reported his mom was scheduled for a heart operation on the 22nd if she improved, but she did not. From a letter Feb. 14: "Well, Mom had a slight heart attack last night. I had the doctor with her at 2:30 this morning and he stayed over an hour with her. Boy, if I lose her I think I will go crazy. I don't know what I would do without her as she is all I have in the world."

Luckily for Phelps, the Dallas crew still had the advantage. From the letter three days earlier, about the Feb. 10 shows: "In Dallas, Tony and I worked in the main event and had a very good match. We worked another return match for next week. I think I got $60 for last night. Well, the other bunch only had 640 paid admissions last night. They had Mr. Moto and Ray Gunkel on top. We had between twenty five hundred and three thousand people so our house went up and there's (sic) down. Mr McLemore was very happy over the crowd last night and so was Max Bowman."

The pendulum swung back the next week, with Dunn returning on top at the Sportatorium and with McShain defending the NWA World Junior Heavyweight title against Starr on top of a return between Moto and Gunkel. From a Feb. 18 Phelps letter: "Last night I worked here in Dallas and I got $40. I worked here with Jack O'Brien and then went back for the six man tag match. ... Well, the other bunch had a good house last night. I don't know just how big it was but I heard they had fifteen hundred people there at Pappy's. I think we had the same amount also."

Phelps remained critical of his side's world champion. "Roy Dunn and Silent Hubert had the worst match I ever seen. It was terrible. Dunn went over two straight falls. The six man tag match was a wild one. Lots of heat."

The Thursday shows were staying steady at a lower rate than the traditional Tuesday nights. Wrote Phelps on Feb. 20: "I worked here in Dallas last night with Silent George Hubert in the main event and I got $25. I got disqualified in

Credits:
1) Dallas Rasslin' program, 1953, Greg Klein Collection
2) Rainbow Sound Records, 1968, "I Wrestled With God!: Conversion Testimony Of Evangelist Tommy Phelps"
3) Signiture on letters to Jack Pfefer, courtesy of Jack Pfefer Collection at Father Theodore Hesburgh Library, University of Notre Dame

the third fall. It was a very good match McLemore said." The personal news was also dim as Mother Phelps "had another attack" and her health was affecting her son's mental well being as well.

The day before the Feb. 24 show, Phelps wrote to say he had hired a woman to be with his mom three days a week "as I can't afford to use her for any more than that as I have to give her five dollars a day and that runs into a lot of money after a while." Pappy's featured Bull Curry beating Big Humphrey and Alo Leilani and Al Costello beat Cyclone Anaya. The Sportatorium had Dunn beating Jack O'Brien in two straight falls and Jack Kennedy and Johnny Dobbs in a rematch. Phelps told Pfefer he thought Pappy's promoter Norman Clark was papering his crowd. "They have been mailing out a lot of passes to these shows. I don't think they have made any money at all except for the television money."

Leo Voss jumped back to the Dallas office to begin March. A popular former wrestler, Voss got billing as the referee for a third match between Kennedy and Dobbs, and a battle between Phelps and O'Brien. From the next day's letter: "I worked here in Dallas last night with Jack O'Brien and I went over on a disqualification. It was two out of three falls. He took the first and I took the second fall. I got $40 for the match and also $20 for the television filming of the match. I am working here again tomorrow night in a tag team match in a double main event. ... Well, the other bunch had eleven hundred people last night and we had nineteen hundred people. Leo Voss came back over with us last night and for good so he says." Phelps signed off by saying he was taking his mother to the hospital for more tests, but "the doctor said there isn't a damn thing he can do for her until her heart gets better as they can't operate as long as her heart is bad."

The next week, Pappy's had Bull Curry and Ray Gunkel on top while the Sportatorium had Phelps against Johnny Dobbs. Thursday, March 12, a six man headlined with Johnny Dobbs, Buddy Farmer and Chuck Simmons beating Sammy Baldwin, Albert Foreman and Jack Kennedy. Phelps wrote Pfefer that night filled with news and optimism: "I worked here on top Tuesday and got $40. I worked on top with Johnny Dobbs and Leo Voss was the referee. Dobbs took the first fall and I took the second and in the third fall they stopped it and called it a no contest. I am working here in Dallas again in a six man tag match. Well, Mr. McLemore has Fort Worth coming over on his side starting next Monday a week and also a couple of more clubs in a couple of weeks. So, it looks like Ed is going to win his battle after all. He is going to have four or five clubs running a week and he said later on he is going to start some more towns." Phelps told Pfefer he had paid about $600 in medical bills for his mother, and he was going to stop going to Kansas for the time being. So, the added Texas dates were something he needed.

For another Dallas boy, Adkisson, the Dallas office had a different request. From Phelps on March 14: "Well, Jack, Mr. McLemore and Mr. Maurice Beck ask (sic) me again if I had written you about Jack Adkisson and I told them I had. So, they said if you could use the boy they would be very glad to send you any information you might want about the boy as they were very interested in getting the boy started off right. He has pictures to send if you are interested and he also has a car. I told you he weighed 225. Well, I was wrong he weighs 250 pounds and no fat and he is six foot three inches tall."

TOMMY PHELPS
. . . unusual apparel

Phelps Wrestles 400-Pound Bear In Mat Special

Tommy Phelps, who tips the scales at [illegible], will take on 400-pound Victor, a wrestling bear, in a special feature of the Monday night card at the Key City Sportatorium.

In the main event, [illegible] and Doug Lindsey will tangle in a best two of three falls or 60-minute limit bout.

Haystack Muldoon and The Scorpion will also go for the best two of three falls or 60 minutes. Haystack weighs in at [illegible] and the Scorpion at [illegible].

Al [illegible] will referee.

Adkisson followed up with his own letter March 17: "I have worked out with Nature Boy several times and he tells me that I have got what it takes to make a good worker if given the chance. I have now had quite a few matches and am definitely determined to stay in the wrestling profession."

Pfefer replied he had no room for the newcomer at the moment, but Adkisson wrote again March 27: "I would like to repeat that I am very anxious to come with you for the simple reason that Mr. McLemore, whose judgment I trust completely, says that I can learn more under you in a year than I would learn five years anywhere else in the country. P.S. I had a match with Tommy last night, and I must say he is one of the best that I have ever worked with." By June, Adkisson was working for Pfefer ally Tony Santos in New England.

Phelps also wrote March 27, but with news his mom had gotten worse and he was cutting back on his dates. "I worked here in Dallas Tuesday and got $40. They put me over Johnny Dobbs. I also got $20 for television filming Tuesday. I am working with Roy Dunn next Tuesday on top here in Dallas. I received your letter today. I am glad your (sic) doing such great business. Keep up the great business. I am working in Fort Worth on Monday with Elephant Boy and Jack Kennedy is working with Roy Dunn. Well, Jack my mother's doctor finally told me yesterday that she is dying a slow death. She has that liver trouble and it's slowly killing her. He said she might live a month or six months as it gets you all at once and you never know when it will come. So you see Jack I'm not exactly having a picnic being home. It's heartbreaking for me thinking I'm not going to have her too much longer."

Although Phelps claimed victory for his mentor, the reality was more complicated and would stay that way throughout the 18-month battle, and for decades to follow. According to McLemore, in 1952, the Tuesday night shows at the Sportatorium averaged 5,500 fans a week, making Dallas the top wrestling city in the state. In spring 1953, a good week meant 4,000 fans spread over three shows, with one belonging to the competition. For McLemore, holding his own, even maintaining a small advantage in crowd size while getting over a new roster of stars, was an accomplishment, but not a profitable one.

In Fort Worth, North Side Coliseum promoter and concessions magnate R.G. McElyea switched his Monday shows to the McLemore side in early-March. A Monday in Fort Worth was a much better trip for Phelps than going to Kansas. April 1: "I worked here in Dallas last night with Roy Dunn. I got $45 for my pay off and I got $20 for television filming. I worked in Fort Worth Monday and got $35. I worked with the Elephant Boy. Mr. McLemore is really treating me fine and so is Mr. Beck. Ed said my match with Dunn was the best that he has had here. Dunn hasn't been getting over at all as he won't register for anybody but last night he did take a couple of bumps for me. Even though it is the best showing he has made the match wasn't what the people are used to seeing down here. They like action and plenty of it but you can't give it to them unless the other guy is willing to do his share. One fellow can't do it all! Tony and I had a wild match in Fort Worth. The promoter was crazy about it. Dunn worked with Kennedy in Fort Worth and Kennedy never got a hold. Dunn was all over him and everything Jack did Roy wouldn't sell it. So you can imagine what kind of a match they had. Well, Jack Adkisson told me last night he had wrote you again the other day. He is really wanting to get started regular in this business and he says from what he has heard about you from McLemore, Jack O'Brien and myself that he is really set on working for you if you can (find) room for him."

April 3, Phelps reported good matches Thursday but no changes in finances: "I worked here in Dallas last night (Thursday) and got $25. I worked with Jack O'Brien and we had a terrific match. We went three falls to a draw. Kennedy worked with John Dobbs in the other three fall match. Kennedy won on a disq. Next Tuesday they have Frankie Murdoch and the Elephant Boy on top and they have the girls and also a tag match Jack O'Brien and Roy Graham against Jack Kennedy and myself plus two other matches. Pappy's Showland has Duke Keomuka and Bull Curry on top."

Aug 8, Phelps wrote with news from both Fort Worth and Dallas: "I worked in Fort Worth Monday night and got $50. We had a tourneyment (sic) to see who would work with Roy Dunn next Monday. I won my first and second match and in the third match which was the last match of the night I missed a tackle and Jack O'Brien won the tourneyment so he works with Dunn next week in Fort Worth. Last night here in Dallas I got $35. I worked in the tag match and my partner got beat. The Elephant Boy beat Frankie Murdock in the main event and next week the Elephant Boy works with Roy Dunn here in Dallas on top. Well, Jack I seen Rudy Soda last night and he didn't have to (sic) much to say for a change."

Phelps had more bad news April 14: "Please excuse me for not writing sooner but as usual my mother has been having some bad attacks lately and I've been sitting up with her night after night. I thought I had lost her the other night as she was really having some bad pains. I had the doctor with her at 3:30 in the morning. Well, Jack, I worked in Fort Worth last night and I got $35. I worked with Johnny Dobbs and I went over. We had a good match. Roy Dunn worked with the Demon Jack O'Brien and Dunn went over two straight falls as usual. Here in Dallas tonight I'm working with Roy Graham in the semi- final and Roy Dunn is working with the Elephant Boy in the main event. The other bunch have Duke Keomuka and Bull Curry back on top again tonight at Pappy's Showland. ... I've really been losing sleep lately staying up with my mother all the time. I've just about lost my mind worrying about her all the time!"

The next day, Phelps gave more details: "I worked here in Dallas last night in the semifinal against Roy Graham. We worked a return for next week. I got $35 plus $20 for T.V. filming. Roy Dunn beat Tony two straight falls in the main event." (Pfefer underlined the sentence about Dunn and Elephant Boy in red ink.) "Jack, in your letter you said you wondered why I didn't write you all the news, well, they don't say anything to me and I didn't know anything about Montana until last night when I heard that Mara Duba and George Valentine had gone there for a few weeks. I also know you like to know what's going on, but if they don't say anything how am I to know what's cooking? I haven't heard hardly a thing lately except that San Antonio and Corpus Christi are opening up on the 27th and 28th and I am sure you already knew about that without me telling you. ... Mr. McLemore has been treating me very good and so has Mr. Beck. My mother is still the same in very poor condition."

The next letter from Phelps is dated April 24: "I worked in Fort Worth Monday and got $25. I worked with Joe Venice and I went over. Tuesday I worked here in Dallas and I got $40 plus $20 for T.V. filming. I worked with Roy Graham in the main event and I went over on a disq. ... I am working in San Antonio Monday and Tuesday I am in Corpus Christi. You wanted to know how much a week I am making since I've been home. Well, its been about $100 or $125 per week some times less and a couple of times a little more but as a whole just about $100 or $125 per week. There was three or four weeks when I only made $60 or 65 on account of me not being able to go to Wichita or some other town on account of mother's condition. Well, Jack I heard that Mr. McLemore was trading boys with Montana territory and he also got some boys from Chicago from (Karl) Pojello. Joe Vinca, Tony Steele and Al Rossi was the boys he got from Chicago and what stinkers they are. I am working here tonight in Dallas in a tag match. They changed nights from Thursday to Friday last week. It was terrible. Billy Sandow killing himself wasn't it. I guess he was a little nuts at times."

And with that, in late April, Tommy Phelps and his "Your boy Izzy" letters to Jack Pfefer stop. Or, at the least, they are not in the collection at Notre Dame's Hesburgh Library. The next letters from Phelps, often signed with his real name, are from 1955, and include wedding and birth announcements. Mother Phelps lived to see her grandchildren. She died in the 1960s.

Considering what is still to come in the war, and what is about to happen in April and May, it is an inopportune time to lose the narration. However, given the dramatic events in Dallas of late April and early May, 1953, the newspapers and the promoters were able to carry the storyline forward without our boy Izzy.

A bridal shower
Is being planned
Sure hope that you
Will be on hand!

Marjorie Phelps
Feb 21,1955
8 oclock
218 N Marsalis
Ann Blood

JACK IZZY Got married
TO A SWEET GIRL

IZZY BECKER

I'VE NEWS FOR YOU--

I ARRIVED Oct 25, 1956

I WEIGHED 6 LBS 13½

MY NAME IS Mark Bradley Phelps

MY PARENTS ARE Marjorie & Tommy Phelps

PRO WRESTLING TERRITORY FACT SHEET

EAST TEXAS (FRITZ/BLANCHARD/BOESCH)

SAMPLE WEEK	
MON 11/1	FORT WORTH
TUE 11/2	DALLAS
WED 11/3	AUSTIN
	SAN ANTONIO
THU 11/4	BEAUMONT
	CORPUS CHRISTI
FRI 11/5	HOUSTON
SAT 11/6	DEL RIO
	KILLEEN
SUN 11/7	--

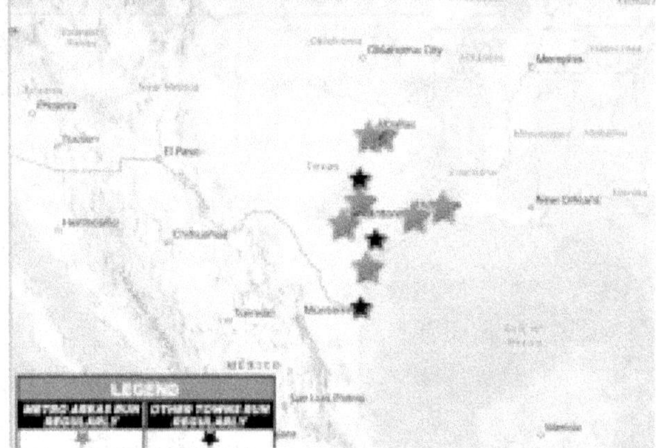

Credits:
1) Al Getz/Charting the Territories, 1971 Map of Texas loop
2) TourTexas.com map

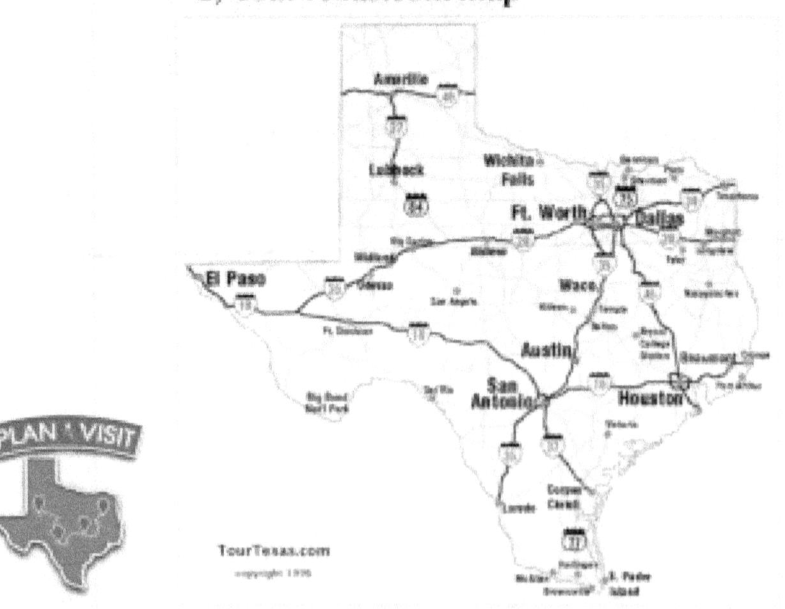

6

The War Expands

In the past decade, the work of wrestling historians to document the day-to-day, week-by-week quality of the professional territory system has produced some amazing results. Led by retired statistician/historian Al Getz and his Charting the Territories brand, the scope of the system is now visible in a way it wasn't previously.

Recently, while looking at Getz's work on Texas in the 1970s, something struck me. The map of the wrestling territory for the state is pretty much identical to the way it looked in the 1930s when the system was established.

So, when Dallas promoter Ed McLemore decided to start staging the 1953 war on multiple fronts, what happened in April 1953 isn't surprising. It is a mirror of what happened in Texas in 1929 and the 1930s. For Morris Sigel, San Antonio and Corpus Christi becoming weekly towns complemented his territory and Dallas and Fort Worth were the completion of the main part of the loop.

For Ed McLemore, with Fort Worth set on Mondays — outdrawing the Dallas shows at least at first — and more talent coming in to supplement the workers he had gotten over that spring, completing the loop was crucial.

According to a *Dallas Morning News* article April 23: "Ed McLemore, Dallas promoter, said today he was opening at San Antonio Monday and Corpus Christi Tuesday in direct competition with Morris Sigel, Frank Burke and Karl Sarpolis, operators of the Texas Wrestling Agency, a booking operation in Houston."

Mat Shows Continue Argument This Week

[illegible]

Bollas, Rito In Main Event At Town Hall

[illegible]

Doubleheader Set For New Diamond

[illegible]

Double Header Opens Casino Card Tuesday

[illegible]

Credits:
1) Corpus Christi Caller, April 26, 1953

The *Corpus Christi Caller-Times* picked up the story with the headline "Wrestling Row Expected to Reach Here Next Week" and inserted a paragraph about the competition locally. Barney Myers promoted for Sigel on Thursdays at the Town Hall venue, but the article said no one had yet picked up a license to promote against him. Jack Irwin and George Schepps were local businessmen mentioned as possible promoters. Within a few weeks, Irwin would open up on Tuesdays at the Casino Arena. A former boxing promoter that owned a liquor store, Irwin's shows would be staged two days ahead of Myers' shows.

"It is retaliation against Sigel and associates for opening up a wrestling show in Dallas in competition with McLemore Jan. 4. Until then Sarpolis was associated with McLemore in the Dallas promotion, being McLemore's matchmaker. Fort Worth, which had been under the TWA banner, joined forces with McLemore March 2. The McLemore alignment now is Dallas, Fort Worth, Wichita Falls, Tyler, San Antonio and Corpus Christi and McLemore said he was going into Waco and Houston soon. The TWA group, which is in the National Wrestling Alliance, which McLemore now shuns, has had wrestling at Dallas, Austin, Corpus Christi, Waco, Galveston, Beaumont, Houston, San Antonio, Raymondville and McAllen, and is reportedly opening at Port Arthur Monday."

The article closed with discussion of the finances of the war thus far. "McLemore said he was not losing any money — in fact was making some — through his concessions and film but that he wasn't realizing a profit on the wrestling itself because the crowds were not big enough. McLemore uses independent wrestlers. The TWA group uses those from the NWA which most promoters in the country are associated with. Sarpolis said his group was making some money in Dallas."

Three days later, the *Corpus Christi Caller-Times* followed up with an article on the local developments. "Town Hall wrestling promoter Barney Myers, who is facing competition here as the Texas-wide wrestling war spread to Corpus Christi, announced yesterday that his affiliation with the Texas Wrestling Agency in Houston will bring some 30 to 40 of the top boys in the mat game here this year.

"At the same time, Jack Irwin, who says he has been assured a state promoter's license for wrestling here, promised an equally lengthy lineup of wrestlers for the cards he intends to stage at the Casino, Lexington and Weber Road, starting Tuesday at 8:30 p.m. Myers' mat shows continue at the regular 8:30 p.m., Thursday spot at Town Hall."

Rito Romero headlined against George Bollas on the Town Hall Show on April 30, while Big Humphrey and Duke Keomuka matched up in the semifinal. On April 28, the McLemore crew debuted in Corpus Christi with Elephant Boy and Johnny Dobbs in the main event and Rose Marie Alvarez and Connie O'Conner as a special attraction. Tommy Phelps worked against Sonny Baldwin in a preliminary match.

The article said the McLemore side claimed their wrestlers had been kept from working for "the syndicate" and that the new shows would expose fans to better action. Myers countered with a list of performers he would be bring in over the year: Ray Gunkel, Verne Gagne, Louis Thesz, Mr. Moto, Danny McShain, "Wild Red" Berry, Bronko Nagurski, the Dusek Brothers, Babe and Chris Zaharias, Billy Varga, Dutch Hefner, Carlos Moreno, Mr. America, "Wild Bill" Longson, Baron Leone and Mildred Burke and her troupe.

"Talent will be my answer to the local competition," Myers said.

The piece also noted the jump of Leo Voss, who was in town to set up Irwin's matches. "When I was with the syndicate, they used to call me one of the five best referees in U.S. wrestling," he said. "Now the boys in Houston call me 'an oversized midget'."

The story ended with the focus on the world heavyweight championship conflict between the champions of the two groups. The paper called him Jack Dunn, not Roy, and noted the dispute between him and Lou Thesz. "Such a match hasn't developed and both sides in the mat war are advancing a battery of reasons why not."

In San Antonio, going to war meant going up against the Livengood-Brown team, no easy task. Dorathy Livengood had been in the ticket office for San

10-B CORPUS CHRISTI TIMES, Wednesday, April 29, 1953

Record Crowd of 2500 Sees 'Wrestling War' at Casino

The "wrestling war" came to town last night and before the Casino Arena show ended just about everything had happened.

The ring ropes collapsed in the final of five bouts.

A record crowd, estimated by police as between 2300 and 2500, saw the show, and about 300 got tired of bucking a late line of ticket buyers and went back home.

Announcer Fails To Show

The regular announcer didn't show up, and a state boxing and wrestling official—Harry Friedman—took over the "mike."

The record crowd stuck around after the ropes had become feeble and until the third fall of the best-of-three closing match had been battled in the center of the ring.

The ropes gave way during the Elephant Boy-Tony Olivas and Johnny Dobbs finals. Dobbs won the first fall with a "choke hold." The Elephant Boy won the second with a double crab after both boys had got so rough that, according to Referee Lee Voss, "the ropes wouldn't stand the beating."

The Elephant Boy won the third fall with a body slam, in the center of the ring.

In the other feature, Connie O'Connor won two of three falls from Kitty Faye. The ropes had not been weakened by that time, but the girls "skipped" them and played "catch" outside the ring until Voss coaxed them back where they belonged. The bout was a crowd-pleaser.

So were the "warm ups" that saw Nature Boy Tommy Phelps and Sonny Baldwin kick and toss each other around to a draw; and also saw Enrique Marba win over Buddy Farmer on a foul.

The Nature Boy and Farmer won over Marba and Baldwin in a tag team match.

The bouts, promoted by Jack Irwin, were the first here in some time in which wrestlers tied up with the Sigel-McLemore Syndicate were not used.

Stable of Independents

Irwin is featuring wrestlers furnished by McLemore, who broke with Sigel and lined up a stable of "independents." The stable includes Chili Raye, who challenged Connie O'Connor, the winner of the girls' bout.

"We just didn't figure on the last minute rush for tickets, Irwin said today, "and next Tuesday we will make better arrangements for the handling of the crowd, no matter how late they come."

Dizzy Davis At Casino; Quits Sigel Syndicate

"Dizzy" Davis, one of the Sigel wrestling syndicate's top attractions has jumped to the McLemore circuit and will wrestle at the Casino tonight.

Casino Promoter Jack Irwin made that announcement late this morning. Davis will wrestle Jack Kennedy, substituting for the Great Van Duke.

Lee Voss, who will referee tonight's bouts quoted Davis as saying: "I'm tired of being pushed around." Voss said Davis had been a syndicate top card for about 15 years. Voss also said Davis is the "first big name" to quit the Sigel chain since Sigel and McLemore tangled in a Texas wrestling war.

Irwin also announced that the ring was "too high" last week and had been lowered a foot for tonight's bouts. He also said that he has set up three ticket windows, instead of one. At the first show, about 400 fans wearied of bucking the ticket line and went home. Irwin also said a section will be reserved for Negroes, and that free bus service will be given to and from the arena. Buses will leave the [illegible] Navy Bus Terminal at 7:30.

Here's the card:

Elephant Boy vs. Nature Boy in the feature. Jack O'Brien and Louis Martinez in the semifinal. Jack Kennedy and Dizzy Davis in the prelim. Buddy Farmer and Nacho [illegible] in the second prelim.

The winners of the two prelims

Holman Hearing Is Adjourned

NEW YORK, May 5 (AP) — A three-man committee of the board of higher education yesterday adjourned until May 26 the trial of Nat Holman, longtime basketball coach of City College of New York, and two other suspended faculty members of the institution.

The other suspended members are Frank S. Lloyd, chairman of the faculty athletic committee, and assistant basketball coach Harry Sand. They are accused of "conduct unbecoming a teacher and neglect of duty."

The charges arose from the college basketball fix scandals of

Credits:

1) Corpus Christi Times, April 29, 1953

2) Corpus Christi Times, May 5, 1953

LIVENGOOD - BROWN ENTERPRISES
The Wrestlethon
405 E. Josephine
San Antonio, Texas

Antonio wrestling almost since the beginning, and her husband, matchmaker Frank Brown, settled into San Antonio as a main eventer in 1944 and never left. In 1947, they built their own building, the Wrestlethon, and ownership had its privileges financially.

To counter them, McLemore recruited Bob Kline, who booked the Municipal Auditorium for Monday, April 27. According to the next day's *San Antonio News*, 3,165 fans attended the event, paying $2,963.85, to see Elephant Boy beat Nature Boy in three falls.

Wednesday, April 29, at the Wrestlethon, Rito Romero and Bud Curtis worked the main event, with Duke Keomuka against Miguel Guzman and Bull Curry against George Bollas underneath. Dizzy Davis opened the show against Aldo Bogi.

As the war took on new fronts, an old one took on great focus as challenges about the true world champion began to circulate. Whatever he lacked in showmanship, Dunn had a reputation as a shooter and the TWA group wasn't going to match him with Thesz, the traveling champ. Instead they offered Ray Gunkel, which led to grandstand challenges back and forth. The Dallas group even proposed for Dunn to take both men in one night.

The Dallas group took out an ad, but instead of listing upcoming matches, they touted Dunn's credentials and challenged the TWA standard bearer. "Wrestling promoter makes $1,000 challenge," read the headline, with a subhead of, "Wants truth to answer of who is real champion."

"The question of who is the real World's Heavyweight Champion has been asked many times of Ed McLemore, Dallas wrestling promoter. Just as often

WRESTLING

CASINO ARENA

Lexington Blvd. & Weber Road

Every Tuesday Night

MIDGETS-MIDGETS-MIDGETS

Sonny Boy Cassidy
vs. Irish Jackie
(1 Fall—30 Minutes)

RETURN BY
PUBLIC DEMAND
6-man Rassle Royal

Ray Piret — Wally Dusek
Sammy Baldwin—Dizzy Davis
Benito Mata—Buddy Farmer
All six men in the ring at one time in a battle to a finish

(Leo Voss, Referee)

Ray Piret "The Flying Dutchman"

MAIN EVENT
DIZZY DAVIS vs RAY PIRET
(2 out of 3 falls — 90 minute time limit)

2 Preliminary Matches
SAMMY BALDWIN vs WALLY DUSEK
(1 Fall — 30 Minutes)
BENITA MATA vs BUDDY FARMER
(1 Fall — 30 Minutes)

Tickets on Sale: 714 Kinney—Phone 4-5414
Horseshoe Inn, Lexington Blvd. — Prince's Drive-Inn, Port-Ayers
JACK IRWIN, PROMOTOR — ADM. PRICE: 75c—$1.00—$1.25
Plus Tax
GENERAL ADMISSION .... 50c Tax. Incl.

Team Match Tops Wrestling At Town Hall

Dizzy Davis, Nature Boy Meet at Casino

Houston Schools Agree

WRESTLING WAR FIGURE CHANGES SIDES AGAIN

DALLAS, May 30 (AP)—Karl Sarpolis returned to the Ed McLemore fold today in the latest developments of a wrestling war going on in Dallas between McLemore, long-time promoter here, and the Texas Wrestling Agency of Houston.

Sarpolis was associated with McLemore for 14 years in the operation of Dallas wrestling, but he was a partner in the Texas Wrestling Agency and pulled away from McLemore when the TWA entered a rival promotion in Dallas.

But Sarpolis said he had resigned as matchmaker for the rival promotion and also would give up his interest in the Texas Wrestling Agency.

Sarpolis said he left McLemore last January when the Dallas promoter quit the National Wrestling Alliance. "But after seeing in recent weeks the methods employed by the Alliance in forcing McLemore to the wall, I decided McLemore was right," Sarpolis declared.

He added that "a lot of wrestlers are now leaving the Alliance and we'll get the rest for our mat cards."

McLemore has opened rival promotions to the Texas Wrestling Agency in San Antonio and Corpus Christi.

Credits:
1) May 26, 1953 ad for Jack Irwin promoted show in Corpus Christi
2) Corpus Christi Caller, May 31, 1953, with stories about both promotion's shows
3) Corpus Christi Caller, May 11, 1953

Mat War Spreads To San Antonio

SAN ANTONIO, Texas, April 15 (AP).—San Antonio gained a second wrestling promoter this past week with Bob Kline taking out a license.

Kline will open his weekly shows April 27 in the Municipal Auditorium. He will work with Ed McLemore of Dallas.

San Antonio's other promoter is Dorathy Livengood, who has staged regular attractions for the past several years.

WRESTLING

AT THE AIR-CONDITIONED
MUNICIPAL AUDITORIUM
Mon., May 4, 8:30 P.M.

MAIN EVENT
"ELEPHANT BOY"
(TONY OLIVAS)
vs
JACK KENNEDY

SEMIFINAL
JACK O'BRIEN
vs
"NATURE BOY"
(TOMMY PHELPS)

TAG TEAM MATCH
CHARLES SIMMONS and
"BUDDY" FARMER vs
ENRIQUE MARBA and
BENITO MATA

TICKETS: Mun. Aud.—G-7101
PRICES: $1.00, $1.50, $2.00

SAN ANTONIO NEWS MONDAY, MAY 25, 1953 11

Kline Mat Show At San Pedro

[illegible]

Credits:
1) Dallas Morning News, April 16, 1953
2) May 4, 1953 ad for Bob Kline show in San Antonio
3) San Antonio Evening News, May 25, 1953

says McLemore, the fans want to know why he doesn't match Roy Dunn vs. Lou Thesz for a world's heavyweight title bout. For those who are not familiar with the fact, Roy Dunn defeated Everett Marshall for the championship and the only recognized title belt in a championship match in Wichita, Kan., on Nov. 1, 1940. Since that time, he has defeated all worthy challengers. Among his victims is Lou Thesz, one of the present-day crop of title claimants. Thesz is associated with a St. Louis wrestling group which has refused to employ Roy Dunn's services because Dunn won't take orders. Thesz meets only Alliance stooges, many of whom he has beaten many times. The National Wrestling Alliance is a self-serving organization who named its champion behind closed doors in a meeting in September of 1949. Dunn won his title in the ring. This Tuesday, McLemore's opposition has announced a Texas Heavyweight Championship bout between Ray Gunkel, alleged Texas Heavyweight Title Holder, and Duke Keomuka. Promoter Ed McLemore announces that he will give $1,000 in cash to anyone able to get the synthetic champion, Lou Thesz, and the winner of the Texas Heavyweight Championship bout Tuesday night to meet Roy Dunn. Dunn agrees to beat both alleged champions in the same night and to donate his share of the purse that night to any reputable charity." The ad ended with another headline, "Mat Fans! Don't Be Fooled Again!"

The *Dallas Morning News* picked up on the challenge, too. April 17, they printed the McLemore dare: "Some spice was added to the local wrestling war Thursday when Promoter Ed McLemore offered $1,000 to anyone who could arrange a match between Roy Dunn and two wrestlers of the opposing camp, Lou Thesz and the winner of the Ray Gunkel-Duke Keomuka scrap next Tuesday night."

"Dunn offers to beat both of them the same night," McLemore said, "and he will give his proceeds to charity. The match can be staged at either my place, the Sportatorium, or at Pappy's Showland."

A week later, the paper printed the response "Wrestling showdown seen near" from Norman Clark and the TWA group: "Norman Clark, who promotes wres-

Business Picks Up With Wrestlers

WARNING: Look for Texas' red-hot wrestling war to get a little warmer in the next few weeks and it may mean more fireworks here in San Antonio.

Dizzy Davis, that old Houston rebel, already has deserted Morris Sigel's camp to sign up with Ed McLemore's syndicate, which supplies mat talent for Bob Kline's Municipal Auditorium shows, and we hear that is only the beginning.

The grapevine is telling that Doc Sarpolis, one of Sigel's partners at Houston, is about to sell out his interests and possibly switch uniforms. George Bollas, one of the Houston combine's head-liners, makes his debut for McLemore in Dallas next week, and Duke Keomuka, always a star attraction as a villain, plans to make the jump within the next month.

This is Davis' second jump from the Sigel ranks. A couple or three years ago he tried to open up his own promotional business but faded quickly after his Houston home burned down.

Now McLemore has lost his Dallas site, the Sportatorium, by fire, but is still making long range plans to stay in business.

Looks like a long, hot summer coming up, in more ways than one.

Ellis Bashara on Kline Mat Card

Ellis Bashara, one of the toughest matmen in the nation, will make his first appearance on Promoter Bob Kline's Monday wrestling program at Municipal Auditorium.

Bashara, a former Oklahoma U. football star, comes in against Jack Adkisson in one of the preliminary matches. New faces dominate the prelims, with Bill Steldum and Dave Brookshire opening the program.

Topping the card is a co-main event with Dizzy Davis matched against Jack O'Brien, and Lou (Mr. Mexico) Martinez facing Tommy (Nature Boy) Phelps. Each bout is two out of three falls.

A special event sends the midgets into action. Diamond Jim swapping grips with Farmer Pete. They go one fall, no time limit.

+++

Jameson 2nd At Reading

READING, Pa., June 5 —UP— Defending champion Betsy Rawls

Credits:
1) San Antonio Evening News, Johnny Janes column, May 6, 1953
2) San Antonio Evening News, June 5, 1953

tling at Papy's (sic) Showland, offered to match Texas Heavyweight Champion Ray Gunkel against world title claimant Roy Dunn, who wrestles for rival promoter Ed McLemore. 'Dunn challenged Gunkel to a bout last week before he won the Texas championship from Duke Keomuka, and we are ready to accept that challenge,' Clark said. 'I doubt if Dunn will show up, but Gunkel will pin him in five minutes if he does.' McLemore, who was in Tyler promoting a show Thursday when informed of Clark's actions, said there was a misinterpretation of the challenge. 'We said we would wrestle Gunkel and Lou Thesz, the National Wrestling Alliance champion,' McLemore observed. 'If we can't get Thesz, we don't want only Gunkel.' 'We will have Gunkel at Pappy's next Tuesday ready to go against Dunn,' Clark reiterated when informed of McLemore's reply. Clark has circulated several hundred placards and handbills announcing the potential bout. They read: 'Ray Gunkel vs. Roy Dunn (if he shows up)'."

If McLemore's double talk helped Dunn's case, it didn't show up at the box office. According to research by Tim Hornbaker and J. Michael Kenyon, the Sportatorium drew a gate of $440.15 on April 28, with Ray Piret beating Roy Graham on top and Jack O'Brien and Tony Steel over Adkisson and Kennedy in a tag. After beating Elephant Boy on April 14, Dunn left Dallas. The promotion moved on to Piret and other headliners. It even brought in new title holders. Meanwhile, the TWA group apparently had its biggest win at Pappy's, drawing $964.30 for Duke Keomuka beating Dizzy Davis and Rito Romero and Ricki Starr going to a draw.

Still, despite the failed challenge of world champions, the war was escalating and it seems fair to say each side had reasons for optimism and causes for concerns. Then came May. It is not an understatement to say what happened in May 1953 in the wrestling war changed people's lives. However the question was: Would any of it change the outcome of the war?

—The Times Herald Staff Photo

FIRE-SCARRED SHELL of the Sportatorium, Cadiz and Industrial, is shown after an early morning fire destroyed most of the 6,400-seat frame and sheet metal structure. Ed McLemore, promoter of wrestling shows there, said it would be rebuilt. He estimated the cost at $150,000.

FLAMES CONSUME the 6,500-seat Sportatorium where wrestling matches have been a weekly feature for several years. The building also has been the scene of the Big D Jamboree, a hillbilly show, as well as numerous benefits.

Credits:

1) May 1, 1953 Dallas Times Herald

2) May 1, 1953 Dallas Morning News

7
The Fire

On Tuesday, April 28, 1953, two men attended the matches at the Sportatorium with no interest in seeing Ray Piret debut against Roy Graham. According to police and court reports, via the *Dallas Morning News* and the Associated Press, Roy Tatum and William Moncrief attended the matches April 28, with the intent of setting fire to the building. However, the weather was ominous and security spooked them, and they decided to wait. Two days and a few hours later, they returned. Using gas as an accelerant, they torched the Sportatorium.

From the UPI wire story May 1: "Fire destroyed the Sportatorium, a 6,400 seat wrestling and boxing arena in 20 minutes Friday and promoter Ed McLemore charged it was 'definitely a case of arson.'"

The story mentioned McLemore's arson claim several times, but would only confirm that local officials were investigating. "McLemore promised to start rebuilding immediately and said he will start holding open-air wrestling shows on the site within three weeks. He said it would cost $150,000 to replace the building and insurance covered only $52,500 of that."

The story stated the building was owned by The Cadiz Corp., W.T. Cox and William Bond Cox, but McLemore and his partners had a lease. However, the building "had been legally doomed when, last March 27, the appellate court affirmed District Judge Sarah T. Hughes' ruling that one third of the building stood on ground, which according to an old agreement, belonged to the state."

A May 13, boxing match between Jacky Blair and Willie Pep had been moved

The fire rages. Courtesy NBC5/KXAS TV News Collection, University of North Texas Special Collections

to the Will Rogers Coliseum in Fort Worth, the story mentioned in closing, but left a future Dallas wrestling card up in the air.

Another story, this one by the Associated Press, gave more details: "The Sportatorium, home of wrestling here for nearly 20 years, was destroyed by a five-alarm blaze that began at 12:35 a.m., today. Within 40 minutes, only a small portion of the wall around the main entrance remained. Fire Chief C.N. Penn said Ed McLemore, who operated it for many years, told him that the building was insured for $52,000. Night Fire Dispatcher A.C. Crowson reported that more than 100 firemen — many of whom had been off duty — were called out to combat the fire. McLemore told the Associated Press it would take 'at least $150,000 to replace the structure.' He said his watchman told him that the building 'just went pouf ... like an incendiary bomb or something.' No show had been held in the crudely-built structure since Tuesday night's wrestling events. During recent years, thousands besides sports fans had become acquainted with the

Promoter Ed McLemore Charges Arson

Dallas Sportatorium Burns To Ground

DALLAS, May 1 —UP—Fire destroyed the Sportatorium, a 6,400-seat wrestling and boxing arena, in 30 minutes Friday and promoter Ed McLemore charged it was "definitely a case of arson."

Assistant County Fire Marshall T. W. Caraday refused to comment on the arson angle, but said he was investigating. So was Sheriff Bill Decker.

"I think it was definitely a case of arson," McLemore said.

He said that at least one previous attempt had been made to burn the building.

McLemore promised to start rebuilding immediately and said he will start holding open-air wrestling shows on the site within three weeks.

He said it would cost $150,000 to replace the building and insurance covered only $52,500 of that.

C. C. Mooney, special officer at the Sportatorium, said he inspected the building 25 minutes before the fire was discovered and found nothing suspicious.

The fire was discovered at 1 a.m. While McLemore said he thinks it was arson, he said he wasn't accusing anybody.

The Sportatorium, owned by W. T. Cox, William Bond Cox and the Cadiz Corp. already had been legally doomed when, last March 27 the appellate court affirmed District Judge Sarah T. Hughes' ruling that one third of the building stood on ground which, according to an old agreement, belonged to the state.

Deputy Sheriff C. C. Mooney, who serves as the Sportatorium's night watchman, had checked the building 30 minutes before the fire broke out about 12:40 a.m. He was sitting in an automobile with another nightwatchman, J. O. Mitchell when they saw fire and smoke shoot up through the ceiling of the Sportatorium.

BLAIR-PEP FIGHT MOVED FROM DALLAS AFTER FIRE

FORT WORTH, May 1 (P)—The Jacky Blair-Willie Pep fight scheduled for national television May 13 has been shifted from Dallas to Fort Worth's Will Rogers Coliseum.

The shift was made necessary when the Sportatorium in Dallas, original site, was destroyed by fire Thursday night.

Promoter Lew Gray of Dallas and Peter Berlent of the International Boxing Club conferred with Coliseum officials and ticket men today before making the announcement.

Sportatorium Fire Causes Move

Pep-Blair Bout Switched Here for May 13

BY BILL VAN FLEET

It Was Arson, McLemore Says

DALLAS (P)—Ed McLemore, operator of the Sportatorium which burned early today, said he believed the blaze was intentionally set.

DALLAS (P)—The Sportatorium, home of wrestling here for nearly 20 years, was destroyed by a five-alarm blaze that began at 12:25 a.m. today.

Within 40 minutes, only a small portion of the wall around the main entrance remained. Fire Chief C. N. Penn said Ed McLemore, who operated it for many years, told him that the building was insured for $52,500.

Night Fire Dispatcher A. C. Crossan reported that more than 100 firemen—many of whom had been off duty—where called out to combat the fire.

McLemore told the Associated Press it would take "at least $150,000 to replace the structure." He said his watchman told him that the building "just went poof...like an incendiary bomb or something."

No show had been held in the crudely-built structure since Tuesday night's wrestling events. During recent years, thousands besides sports fans had become acquainted with the arena through attendance at hillbilly music shows.

This definitely ended the grunt-and-groan sport at the river bottom location, though the death-knell was legally sounded on March 27 when the appellate court affirmed Dist. Judge Sarah T. Hughes' judgment that the owners of the property would have to clear all structures from the old Trinity River channel.

Judge Hughes found that about one-third of the Sportatorium stood on ground that belonged to the state under an old agreement.

Owners of the sports palace were W. T. Cox, William Bond Cox and the Cadiz Corporation.

Credits:

1) Dallas Morning News, May 1, 1953

2) Fort Worth Star Telegram, May 1, 1953

3) Dallas Times Herald, May 1, 1953

At 12:35 a.m. Friday, May 1, 1953, on the corner of Cadiz and Industrial Boulevard in Dallas, a five-alarm fire consumed the "sports palace" known as the Sportatorium.

Night Fire Dispatcher A. C. Crowson reported that over 100 firefighters were called to help extinguish the fire. The 6,400-seat, one-story stadium was insured for $82,500 according to Ed McLemore, Sportatorium promotor and the head of the Cadiz Corporation that owned the famous sports stadium

Sportatorium destroyed by fire, May 1, 1953. PA76-1/14286.2, from the Hayes Collection, Dallas Public Library

arena through attendance at hillbilly music shows. This definitely ended the grunt-and-groan sport at the river bottom location, though the death-knell was legally sounded on March 27 when the appellate court affirmed Dist. Judge Sarah T. Hughes' judgement that the owners of the property would have to clear all structures from the old Trinity River channel. Judge Hughes found that about one-third of the Sportatorium stood on ground that belonged to the state under an old agreement."

As it turns out, McLemore found another venue and also quickly made plans to rebuild the Sportatorium. By May 5, he had moved his Tuesday show to the Fair Park Livestock Pavilion, more than three miles west of the Sportatorium site. The Thursday show promoted by Maurice Beck became the first casualty of the war, canceled in the aftermath of the fire, although perhaps tellingly, not scheduled the Thursday before the morning of the fire.

In the McLemore group's May 12 program, the situation is summed up in their own words, headlined "Sportatorium Burned Down, New Sportatorium Is Promised, End of Era Inspires New Sports Arena" and the article included new developments, which would change the landscape again: "As this is written, Thursday night, May 7th, we are happy to report to you that workmen have almost entirely cleared away the debris of the old Sportatorium, destroyed by fire last Friday a little after midnight. That means soon, the new Sportatorium will be going up and that we will soon be back at the old location — in a brand new building."

Mid-graph came a bombshell. "Other good news we received today was the tidings that Doc Sarpolis returned as Promoter Ed McLemore's matchmaker." A hastily written story in another page of the program tells of Doc's reasoning for returning. "Looking over the situation, we have a very nice and comfortable location out here at Fair Park for the matches until the Sportatorium is rebuilt. The new arena is well-roofed and it is open-sided. It will be cool all summer, and we can never be rained out, as remote a possibility as that may seem."

McLemore's writing team was long on sentiment and determination: "The Sportatorium was built in the Texas centennial year of 1936. At that time it was a great achievement in the architectural world, so far as arena construction was concerned. It was a Dallas landmark. The blaze that destroyed it in less than 40 minutes will never wipe out the fond memories of the many years of its colorful history. But to serve the selfish interest of some outsiders, the Dallas landmark was destined to go, evidently at any cost. It will be a long time forgetting the old Sportatorium."

The bigger news continued in the article in the back of the program, as one of McLemore's original partners, Doc the matchmaker, resigned his NWA membership, TWA stock and Houston affiliation to return to Dallas. "McLemore-Sarpolis Back Together; Doc vs. NWA" read the headline, with a subhead, "Doc Resigned NWA And TWA: Joins McLemore" and a picture of McLemore that noted he was welcoming Doc back. "'Matchmaker' Karl (Doc) Sarpolis, who once left medical school to become a professional wrestler, and later left professional wrestling to become Promoter Ed McLemore's Dallas matchmaker, is back with McLemore now! Doc's first day of work with McLemore consisted mostly of reviewing past great things in Dallas wrestling history and promising each other greater days for Dallas wrestling fans under a promotion with no fears of any syndicate. Sarpolis' picture in the 'wrestling war' was a perplexing

Down at Ringside . . .

A little over two weeks ago the syndicate had the brazen effrontery to publish a wrestling "card" billing Ray Gunkel against Roy Dunn—"if he shows up." As we told you before this match Roy Dunn did not show up nor will he show for any match with an syndicate stooge or so-called champion unless the syndicate agrees to pit their alleged world champion Lou Thesz against Dunn the same night.

As usual, the syndicate again acted in bad faith with the fans, the paying customers, in advertising a match for which they had no contract and when they well knew would not take place. The fans know that any match must be entered into by both parties and they also know that when a Dunn match with the NWA puppets is finally arranged it will be well publicized by both sides and the daily papers.

Again we say, DON'T BE FOOLED, the syndicate is afraid to let Roy Dunn in the same ring with their "appointed" champion and they will go to any lengths to camouflage the true facts.

Roy Dunn has chased the aging Thesz all over the country only to meet the same runaround he has received in Texas. He will not be forced into any phony elimination meet, nor will he be content with a match against anyone but Thesz. BUT HE WILL MEET GUNKEL OR ANY OTHER WRESTLER THEY NAME ON THE SAME NIGHT HE MEETS LOU THESZ.

Meanwhile, here's a tip on the best way to come to the wrestling matches at the new arena at Fair Park. Merely drive into the big Cotton Bowl parking lot at the south end of the Fair Grounds. Walk through the big center aisle of the live stock barns right on into the Live Stock Pavilion. Thus you will be protected from the weather in case of rain.

The new arena is roofed, but opened-sided and promises to be cool during the coming summer heat. You will find the grandstand seats even more convenient to the ring than the old Sportatorium. And all the conveniences you have been used to at the Sportatorium are on hand at the new location.

Big D Jamboree will also be held every Saturday night at the new location so come on out next Saturday and enjoy the Carlisles in person.

•

Enjoy your best wrestling with Ed McLemore.

Credits:
1) May 12, 1953 Dallas Rasslin' program courtesy of the Rare Books and Special Collections Department, Hesburgh Libraries, University of Notre Dame

one. At first, he thought his place was with the National Wrestling Alliance. With that early conclusion, he stayed with the Houston outfit referred to in the papers as the 'TWA.' Just lately, April 28th to be exact, he severed that connection. Doc stated that his reasons were because of 'foul' tactics. Whatever the outcome of his resignation of the so-called 'wrestling war' Doc was determined to have no more part of the opposition's strategy. It was then that he went to McLemore and asked him if he wanted any help. McLemore was happy to rejoin with Sarpolis — and the combination that had built Dallas into the top mat town of the nation was once again reunited."

Interestingly, the April 28 date means the jump came before the fire, and the dirty tactics are alleged to be the blackballing of McLemore's talent by NWA promoters. "Sarpolis cited the instance of the Alliance 'blackballing' any wrestler who worked for McLemore in opposition to an Alliance promoter. Any wrestler who worked for McLemore was automatically blackballed by all other Alliance promoters — just for wrestling for an honest promoter who wouldn't take orders from the Alliance — an Alliance that is supposed to protect the wrestlers — and the wrestling fans."

The article goes on to talk about talent: A subhead, "To Beat NWA" started the next section. "However, McLemore and Sarpolis intend to prove to the world and to the NWA that top-notch wrestlers are not afraid of the Alliance. Already, even before Sarpolis' arrival, wrestlers such as George Bollas, Frankie and Paul Murdock, Ellis Bashara and Vic Holbrook were enlisting on McLemore's side." McShain, Danny Savich and Duke Keomuka are mentioned as potential jumpers. "The black-balling of such wrestlers was one of the tactics that Sarpolis objected to strenuously. Such tactics that put McLemore's back to the wall have not been enough. What were the other methods that might force McLemore out of the wrestling business? They were strong enough methods to force a man of Sarpolis' character to leave such organizations — but not strong enough to make him quit the fight. A new Sportatorium will arise on the same site of the one burned down, and your favorite wrestlers will be competing there before too long."

The *Houston Post* picked up the story with a headline "Sarpolis Quits Sigel, Joins Rival," for its May 11 edition: "Karl Sarpolis returned to the Ed McLemore fold Sunday in the latest development of a wrestling war going on in Dallas between McLemore and the Texas Wrestling Agency of Houston, headed by Morris Sigel. Sarpolis was associated with McLemore for 14 years in the operation of Dallas wrestling, but he was a partner in the Texas Wrestling Agency and pulled away from McLemore when the TWA entered a rival promotion in Dallas. But Sarpolis said he had resigned as matchmaker for the rival promotion and also would give up his interest in the Texas Wrestling Agency. Sarpolis said he left McLemore last January when the Dallas promoter quit the National Wrestling Alliance. 'But after seeing in recent weeks the methods employed by the Alliance in forcing McLemore to the wall, I decided McLemore was right,' Sarpolis declared. He added that 'a lot of wrestlers are now leaving the Alliance and we'll get the best for our mat cards.' McLemore has opened rival promotions to the Texas Wrestling Agency in San Antonio and Corpus Christi."

In an article in the *Fort Worth Press* on April 27, McLemore spoke about the blacklist. "Sigel and the TWA are getting in their licks, too," he said. "Each week from Houston goes out a blacklist to practically every promoter in the country, naming the wrestlers who have bolted the NWA and are working in this territory for the new agency."

Sigel wrote to Muchnick, telling him his side of the story. Sarpolis told him and Burke he wanted out and would sell his TWA shares to the highest bidder if the partners did not buy him out. Sigel later explained to Muchnick: "We paid him off 100 cents on the dollar on his interest in the booking agency and the next thing I know, Doc is with Mac and McElyea in the competing booking agency."

Despite Doc switching sides, and the promise of more wrestlers following him, it turned out, the only other big jump to occur was Dizzy Davis. Davis showed up at a baseball "party" at the Cotton Bowl, where there was a special

Sportatorium Burned Down; New Sportatorium Is Promised

End of Era Inspires New Sports Arena

Credits:

1) May 12, 1953 Dallas Rasslin' program courtesy of the Rare Books and Special Collections Department, Hesburgh Libraries, University of Notre Dame

wrestling promotion, and left with a bloody nose and the main event spot against Elephant Boy on May 12. Davis switching sides the week of a suspicious fire has to be considered, of course, but the exact date he switched sides isn't clear. As with Ellis Bashara and the others, Davis had a relationship with Sarpolis, and the wrestlers who jumped first may have been part of a coordinated effort that started before Doc's official announcement. In any event, Davis gave the promotion an established Texas headliner for its first trip around the circuit and he made similar dramatic appearances in San Antonio on Monday, May 4, and Corpus Christi on Tuesday, May 5, the latter match advertised ahead of time.

Whatever the date of his decision, Davis did resume his Houston grudges, and he did take some action immediately, filing a complaint with the city of Houston about selective contracts on the City Auditorium. From a May 13 story in the *Houston Chronicle*: "Legality of a contract giving Morris Sigel exclusive rights to the City Auditorium for wrestling shows was challenged Wednesday by wrestler Dizzy Davis. Davis said he would appear before the city council and demand use of the auditorium for wrestling promotions. He wants to stage his wrestling shows on Wednesday nights. Mr. Sigel's (shows are) on Friday nights. Reportedly, Davis is backed by a number of wrestling independents who are determined to cut themselves a piece of the wrestling pie that the Sigel interests have held exclusively here for over 30 years. Law Violation Claim: One of the angles of attack Davis will use is a claim that state liquor license law is being violated. He said the law provides that only one beer license shall be held at one place of business. Davis claims that actually there are two licenses held at the auditorium, one by Sigel and the other by Restaurateur Bill White. Mainly, he claims the city does not have the right to give exclusive right of a public facility to any one person. This means the other promoters are barred from using those facilities for wrestling at any time. Mr. Sigel was issued a five-year contract just over a year ago. Under it, he pays the city $250 a night for every Friday night of the year. Davis said he has checked with Public Properties Director Deering and found there are 28 Wednesday nights open for the remainder of this year.

Applied for Dates: He said he applied for those dates, but that Mr. Deering wrote him a letter telling him the auditorium was 'open to anyone for any purpose except for wrestling.' 'This is the first time anyone has had the nerve to challenge Mr. Sigel's rights to the auditorium,' Mr. Davis said. Mr. Sigel said he was not aware of Mr. Davis' intentions. 'I've got a contract with the city and I assume they will stand by it in good faith,' he said."

The next day, *Chronicle* Sports Editor Dick Freeman wrote about the issue in his "Press Box" column. "I don't know why Sterling (Dizzy) Davis went before City Council Wednesday, asking for the use of the City Auditorium for Wednesday nights for wrestling, unless it was just to muddy up the water, which already is far from clean and blue. 'Dizzy,' the wrestler from Houston, attacked the contract, which the city has signed with Morris Sigel, giving him the sole use for wrestling for several years, in exchange for a guarantee of 50 weekly shows in the building each year. Davis knew it when he appeared. He is part of the organization which is coming in to buck Sigel in the wrestling game in Houston and which is on the losing end of the battle against Sigel and his associates in Dallas. They include Ed McLemore, former partner with Sigel, Frank Burke and Karl Sarpolis in the Dallas operation. When McLemore and Sarpolis broke with Sigel there, Norman Clark, with the backing of Sigel, opened a rival promotion, and now is drawing about twice as much as McLemore, et al."

The column recounted the 1950 battle, and the previous attempt by McLemore and Sarpolis to take the booking office from Sigel. Freeman alleges this is also the point when McLemore made the wrestlers sign the contracts that contributed to the issues with the boys.

"While they were at it, they signed more than a score of wrestlers in Dallas to a contract which would have prevented them from wrestling in any ring in the country without permission of McLemore and his associates. It was worded that they couldn't wrestle any place where there is a telecast or radio broadcast other than Dallas, without that permission. The wrestlers who had signed, and who said they had not received the television cut they had been promised, chal-

Dallas Wrestling

PAPPY'S SHOWLAND WHERE YOU SEE WRESTLERS OF PROVEN ABILITY

Dallas Fans! . Here's the Truth! . Read This Article

. . . . By Prominent Sports Writer Frank Godsoe . . . .

MUSCLE MARKET

By FRANK A. GODSOE

* * *

What Happened When He Didn't Die

Have Memories Like Elephants

* * *

Bonfire Demolished Doomed Building

Credits:

1) May 19, 1953 Dallas Wrestling program, featuring Frank A. Godsoe column, courtesy of the Rare Books and Special Collections Department, Hesburgh Libraries, University of Notre Dame

lenged the contracts and had them thrown out. Now I understand they are ready to demand an accounting of the money they claim is due to them."

Freeman seemed to discount the chances Davis had at city council, saying he wasn't sure why he would try the stunt. As for the rest of the war: "Sigel said today that he was buying Sarpolis' interest in the Texas Wrestling Agency. There is still the matter of the Dallas franchise, which was owned jointly by McLemore, Sarpolis, Sigel and Burke. McLemore just told Sigel and Burke they were out, while Sigel was ill, Morris tells me. You can look for some court action on that, too."

While one week or two of triumphs in Dallas attendance figures did not mean the Houston group was winning the war in Dallas, Freeman's column did show the Sigel group using its press contacts to get its side of the story out. Frank A. Godsoe's May 13 column from the *Houston Press* also reported from the Sigel side, so much so his column was reproduced in the May 19 Dallas Wrestling program from "Pappy's Showland, Where You See Wrestlers of Proven Ability." It was also reprinted by other columnists and papers in the state. "Its fate may never jeopardize the nation's economy, but the life of professional wrestling in Texas hangs in the balance. It not only is big sports business, but an industry which last year grossed $1,708,099 in our state. A war of serious consequences rages at the moment, is increasing in intensity with no solution in sight, and had since December. There doesn't now exist a monopoly in its control, and one never has existed. The biggest man in the business has, for three decades, been the Houston promoter, Morris Sigel."

The next section "What Happened When He Didn't Die" recounts the Dallas story through Houston's eyes. "In 1939, the owner of the Dallas Sportatorium, home of boxing, wrestling and hill-billy music, persuaded Sigel to come to Dallas and reorganize a promotion that had died a natural death. From 1939 to 1952, the promoter of wrestling in Dallas was the Dallas Wrestling Club, composed of Ed McLemore (1/3), Sigel, Karl Sarpolis and Frank Burke, who had 2/9ths each, or two thirds, collectively. Sarpolis and Burke were also equal partners with Sigel in the Texas Wrestling Agency. All of them prospered. In February of last year, Sigel suffered a heart attack which for a time appeared might be fatal. During the period when Sigel battled for his life, an effort was made on the part of McLemore and Sarpolis to move the Texas Wrestling Agency from Houston to Dallas. Sigel recovered, stubborn fellow, and the booking business stayed here!"

The column also put a new spin on the origin of the feud. "During the same period, McLemore and Sarpolis devised a plan and induced such leading stars as Wild Red Berry, Mr. Moto, Cyclone Anaya, Ray Gunkel, world heavyweight champion Lou Thesz and others into signing contracts barring their appearance for any other promoter in the United States permitting televised bouts, for 10 years. They were to be paid $5 for each time a film in which they appeared was sold to a television station for exhibition. The contract contained no provision for the accounting to the wrestlers. McLemore testified in district court in Dallas that the TV take was divided between himself and Sarpolis. He denied, of course, knowledge of what Sarpolis did with the rest of the money. A district court ruling denied them the right to enforce the contracts. That's when the war broke out all over."

"Have Memories Like Elephants" headlined the next section. "Sigel's version is that Sarpolis said, 'Morris, I've wronged you, I'm sorry,' and begged forgiveness. With a tolerance that appears to have bordered on the foolish, Sigel eventually did forgive him, for they remained in business. What about McLemore? He simply declared himself the sole promoter of wrestling in Dallas and struck out on his own. What about the partners? They became interested in, and backed Norman Clark of Galveston who leased Pappy's Showland in Dallas, the city where Sigel, Burke and Sarpolis owned two thirds of the business. The wrestlers remembered that television gimmick, and refused to wrestle for McLemore and appeared for Clark. A connection was made to televise Clark's matches. On the opening night (Jan. 6), the telecast blacked out. The equipment was believed to be tampered with. Clark and Pappy Dolsen, owner of Pappy's Showland, reported telephoned threats and requested police protection. McLemore set up the Southwest Sports Agency to compete with the Texas Wrestling Agency (similar ones in Amarillo and El Paso aren't involved in the war). Competing promotions began in San Antonio and Corpus Christi. The only wrestler TWA had (who was an important attraction) to go to the Southwest agency was Dizzy Davis, who had formed an agency and tried to compete with Sigel as a rival promoter here in 1949. After his venture failed, Davis again began to wrestle for Sigel, headlining many bouts here. As of April 25, Sarpolis pulled out of the Texas Wrestling Agency and allied himself with the rival group. A year ago wrestling in Dallas grossed $236,330.51. Several weeks after Clark's promotion began, McLemore's crowds began to dwindle. Clark's have increased progressively. On Tuesday night, April 28, McLemore drew only $440.15 According to figures of the Texas Labor Commission, which are public records. That week Clark drew $964.30 — more than double. The week before Clark had drawn approximately $1,700."

Finally, in a section headlined "Bonfire Demolished Doomed Building," the talk turned to the fire. This section begins with an odd mistake, dating the fire to Tuesday rather than Friday morning. "On the night of April 28, a fire, apparently of an incendiary nature, destroyed the Sportatorium, owned by W.T. Cox, William Bond Cox and the Cadiz Corporation and leased to McLemore and his partners under sundry agreements since 1939. Insurance in force was reported at $52,500. An interesting fact is that one-third of the ground on which the Sportatorium was located had been ruled as property of the state under a ruling of the district court and affirmed by the Fifth Civil Court of Appeals, March 27. The court ruling already doomed the building. Thirty four nights later, it burned. McLemore simply moved his business into the Dallas Livestock Arena, seating 6,000 people. Since then it has been echoed through the state that McLemore's opposition committed the arson. Nasty charge, huh? What would the Houston faction have to gain? Why, nothing that I can see. Clark was winning the battle for the patronage of Dallas fans. McLemore had a place to move his

Four Men Held In Sportatorium Fire

DALLAS, Aug. 22—(AP)—Four men were under arrest today and three of them have been charged with arson or attempted arson following a 3-month probe of the $150,000 Sportatorium fire here.

Charged with arson in the May 1 blaze were Roy Tatum of Houston and William Theodore (Bill) Moncrief of Aubrey, Denton County.

Alford Huey McCrory, a Louisiana resident, arrested Aug. 14 in California, has been charged with attempted arson at the 6,500-seat arena.

Sheriff Bill Decker of Dallas County said today that the fourth man held was believed to be the person who placed two 5-gallon cans of gasoline behind the sports arena last January in an unsuccessful burning attempt.

Tatum, returned to Dallas Friday night by plane from Chicago by County Fire Marshal Hal Hood, and McCrory both named Moncrief as the man who hired them, Decker said.

Moncrief, an ex-convict with a long record of arrests, late Friday night had refused to make any statements.

Sportatorium Arson Go-Between Is Named

DALLAS (AP)—William Moncrief, 38, of Denton County was pointed to yesterday as the intermediary in a scheme that resulted in the $200,000 Sportatorium fire.

The wrestling arena burned May 1. Moncrief is on trial for conspiracy to burn.

Charges of arson and conspiracy to burn have been filed against Roy Tatum, 38, former food storage worker for a Chicago hotel. Alfred McCrory, 34, former Houston resident, is charged with conspiracy.

Tatum testified he set the fire but said Moncrief proposed the idea and paid him [illegible] to strike the match.

McCrory, Jack Ragsdale of Houston, and William Cook of Houston testified Moncrief had talked to them in January about burning the arena.

McCrory said he almost decided to do it but backed out. He said Moncrief taunted him after he decided not to do it.

Tatum testified he and Moncrief went to matches at the arena and that the latter told him he wanted to "destroy TV films." So far that has been the only indication of a motive for burning the building given in court.

Tatum said Moncrief was a go-between for "somebody else."

"I didn't ask whose money it was and he never told me," Tatum said.

Ragsdale testified Moncrief "wanted to pay me $100 for burning down the Sportatorium" but that he did not accept the offer.

Denton Man Is Sentenced For Conspiracy

Dallas, Tex., Dec. 10 (INS)—William T. Moncrief, a 38-year old Denton County automobile upholsterer, was sentenced to five years in prison after a jury found him guilty of conspiracy to burn the old Sportatorium sports arena in Dallas last May.

No notice of appeal was given by Moncrief's attorney yesterday after the jury returned its verdict finding Moncrief guilty of conspiring with Roy Houston Tatum, who had admitted he set fire to the arena.

The Sportatorium, owned by promoter Ed McLemore, was destroyed by fire May 1, with a loss of some $200,000.

Credits:
1) Dallas Morning News, Aug. 22, 1953
2) Dallas Morning News, Dec. 9, 1953
3) Associated Press story, Dec. 10, 1953

dwindling attractions. This I'm impelled to say about Sigel. His chief fault, from my observations, simply is his tendency to forgive people who have spit in his face. Or it is a fault? In the wrestling business, perhaps it is."

The Sportatorium fire caused a stir among the NWA members, too. Muchnick wrote about it and the Texas war in the May NWA bulletin. "It has been suggested by a member that pending the settling of difficulties in Texas, that the Houston office be dropped from the Alliance rolls and that the Texas people in the controversy work out their own problems," he wrote. "The president thinks that it would be wrong to make such a move as it would drop a member just when he is in trouble and needs the help of those pledged to help him."

Sigel answered his critics in a letter dated May 7, 1953, and sent to all the NWA members. "As I explained to you people at the Chicago meeting ... I had no quarrel with Ed McLemore, (R.G.) McElyea or anyone else," he wrote. "We were partners in Dallas, and were booking the territory. When people desert you, as those people did, there is no question of their being wrong, and that is why you all gave me your pledge of support. If this Alliance is to survive, and to prove to the people in the wrestling business that we will all stick together, now is the time for each and every one of you to prove your loyalty — first, to the organization, and second to me. The situation that has occurred here can occur anywhere. We are pledged to help each other. This is one time when the members of the Alliance can prove themselves and help us here all they possibly can. I am asking for your support, just as I would give you mine, if you were in trouble."

As for the Sportatorium, ultimately, the courts adjudicated the fire and several people did pay for what turned out to be arson. However, the greater question was "Who Done It?" Or, who hired the henchmen who planned and set the Sportatorium fire? That question is still unanswered. His gimmick name was Tony from Houston and his purported goal was to burn the wrestling films, according to court testimony, but in a twist worthy of a wrestling storyline, the films were not in the location Tony's henchmen were told to destroy.

One month before the new Sportatorium opened, the news about the arson broke. From an Associated Press story Aug. 22: "Four men were under arrest today and three of them have been charged with arson or attempted arson following a three-month probe of the $150,000 Sportatorium fire here. Charged with arson in the May 1 blaze were Roy Tatum of Houston and William (Bill) Theodore Moncrief of Aubrey, Denton County. Alford Huey McCrory, a Louisiana resident arrested Aug. 14 in California, has been charged with attempted arson at the 6,500 seat arena. Sheriff Bill Decker of Dallas County said today that the fourth man held was believed to be the person who placed two five-gallon cans of gasoline behind the sports arena last January in an unsuccessful burning attempt. Tatum returned to Dallas Friday night by plane from Chicago by County Fire Marshall Hal Hood, and McCrory both named Moncrief as the man who hired them, Decker said. Moncrief, an ex-convict with a long record of arrests, late Friday night had refused to make any statements." The fourth man, Jack Ragsdale, was also questioned, and did testify, but was not charged.

The next day, the papers reported the confession, or actually, two of them. "Hood quoted Tatum as saying he and a companion started the arena fire after they were offered $150 to do it. Tatum refused to name his companion or why somebody wanted the arena burned. He did say that the payoff was only $100. McCrory, in a five page signed statement, said a man in Houston offered him $100 for the job. He said he came to Dallas with the man but 'chickened out' on the plan when he became frightened." The criminal records of the participants was more obvious in the follow ups. "Houston records show Tatum was arrested here in 1947 for the theft of a motor scooter. He served 90 days in jail for the theft. His home address at that time was Edna. Moncrief's police record includes 28 arrests, many of them in Houston. He was arrested here at least six times in 1952 and was released after investigation which followed each arrest. His record begins in 1931, when he was arrested in El Paso on a misdemeanor theft charge. The only prison sentence shown on his record is a two-year term for burglary in 1940 after serving a year of the sentence."

The men were scheduled for trial in October, but in September the cases were delayed two months. By then, Tatum and McCrory had cut deals and were testifying in Moncrief's trial. Moncrief was fingered as the middle man and local fixer, who solicited Ragsdale, McCrory and finally Tatum, looking for help setting the fire. Tatum testified Moncrief had orders to "destroy TV films" although there were none in the office area they were instructed to burn. The men also cast some light on the timeline, indicating they were approached by Moncrief as early as January of 1953, when the war was fresh and the court ruling necessitating the destruction of the Sportatorium was, too.

William Moncrief at trial. UNT Digital archives

From an Associated Press report Dec. 9: "'Moncrief had been in a car wreck recently and said he couldn't burn it himself,' the witness said, 'because he couldn't run. So, he hired me for half of the $300 to do it.' The two bought tickets to wrestling matches so they could see the interior of the building, Tatum said. As they walked into the structure, he testified, Moncrief pointed to the business office. 'He said the purpose was to burn the front end where the office was located,' Tatum said."

The jury convicted Moncrief and he was sentenced to five years in jail. An appeal failed a year later. The AP story the day of the conviction noted it took the jury only 40 minutes to find Moncrief guilty and he was given the maximum sentence. It also gave more information on his mysterious boss as "the name 'Tony' turned up in testimony. Prosecutor Fred Bruener said 'Tony' was a man higher in the conspiracy than Moncrief. But no further identification was made. Alvin Dalrymple, 32, said he went with Moncrief and Tatum to Houston last May 1 and that they stopped at a grill on Preston Ave. He also testified that Moncrief telephoned a man in Houston named Tony and reported that after the fire everything was alright. Alfred H. McCrory testified Tuesday that Moncrief asked him to set fire to the arena and that Moncrief said he would have to get the money from Tony in Houston.

In early January 1954, the other sentences were handed down. “Light terms given in two arson cases,” the *Dallas Morning News* declared. Tatum got two years each for his two pleas of arson and conspiracy, but received concurrent sentences. McCrory got a two-year sentence for conspiracy to commit arson, but was given probation. Both men had been in jail since August, so they were given credit for time served and McCrory was freed on probation. “Both McCrory and Tatum were state’s witnesses in the Moncrief trial, and, said First Asst. Dist. Attorney Fred Bruner, helped convict Moncrief. Both County Fire Marshal Hal Hood and Bruner recommended that Criminal Dist. Judge Henry King go easy on McCrory and Tatum.”

The article again ends with mention of Tony from Houston. That’s where the “We know who did it” ends and the “Who done it begins.” It is possible there will never be an answer about Tony’s real identity.

Sigel and McLemore, despite their differences, had similar reputations in their cities as civic men, who treated their businesses and their cities with respect. They gave to charities. They supported the arts. Yet, each was known for tough business practices. It isn’t impossible to rule either man out, but Sigel’s involvement isn’t a sure thing, either, especially given the Sportatorium needed to be rebuilt anyway.

The who done it was never solved. It may never be solved. As with any good mystery, in the case of who burned the Sportatorium, there are many suspects, all with motive, means, and some with reputation, to do such a deed. Yet, it is all speculation. The identity of Tony from Houston is still unknown.

— Dallas News Staff Photo

SPORTATORIUM GOES UP AGAIN

Symbolizing the start of construction on a new Sportatorium, Promoter Ed McLemore, left, digs a spadeful of earth at the Cadiz and Industrial site. He gets an assist from a friend, Promoter Jack Pfefer of New York City. The old Sportatorium burned down May 1. The new one, costing $150,000 and seating 6,400, will house its first wrestling show in early September.

Kline Quits Mat Shows

Wrestling Promoter Bob Kline has called an end to his weekly shows here at the Municipal Auditorium. Kline said Saturday night that he had sold his interests to Sidney Balkin, nephew of Morris Sigel.

Siegel is the wrestling czar of Houston and head of the Southwest Athletic Association, controlling factor of the mat game in Texas. It is Siegel who furnishes all talent to the Wednesday night shows in San Antonio.

Kline did not give any reason for quitting but said the "whole deal will be made known tomorrow."

NEW MAT PROMOTER—Bill Lawlor takes over the Friday night wrestling promoter's job this week. The Municipal Auditorium programs were operated by Bob Kline in the past.—News Sportsphoto.

Audi Mat Show On Tonight

A new promotional team takes over the wrestling show in air-conditioned Municipal Auditorium Friday night with the first shot fired by promoter Bill Lawlor and matchmaker Willard Brown being a three-bout program.

A girls tag team match, best two of three falls, headlines the show, with Slave Girl Moola and Mars Bennett teamed against Daisy Mae and Darling Dagmar.

The Mighty Zuma, a South American with an aerial drop kick as his chief stock in trade, makes his first apperanace here against Nature Boy in another two-of-three fall bout.

Lou (Mr. Mexico) Martinez opens the show against El Diablo, another newcomer.

Ticket prices have been scaled at $2 ringside, $1.50 orchestra circle, and $1 balcony. Children under 12 will be admitted free when with

Auditorium Mat Show Tonight

Four "Gentlemen" will have a hard time keeping the limelight in the five events on the Municipal Auditorium wrestling card which starts at 8:30 p.m. Friday night.

Five gal grapplers will be co-featured with the gents in a show that will revolve around a five-girl tagmatch in addition to regulation contests between Mars Bennett and Darling Dagmar and between Slave Girl Moolah and Princess Maritza. Daisy Mae, the gum-chewing hill-billy gets into the act for the tag merry-go-round.

Pedro Martinez, a newcomer from Mexico, goes against John Shaw the rough-house ex-policeman, in one of the men's matches and Argentina Zuma, the leaping Argentinian, faces rugged Jack O'Brien in the other.

Wrestlethon

Rito Romero will have a featured spot in next Wednesday night's semi-final match at the Wrestlethon Arena, Matchmaker Frank Brown announced Friday, but his opponent has not been selected.

Romero earned the No. 2 spot on the weekly card by wrestling Jimmy James to a draw last Wednesday. James won a coin flip after the bout and got the right to take on Andre Drapp, the French star, in the main event.

Romero's bout will be a one-faller with a 30-minute time limit. Drapp and James are billed for two out of three falls in a match having a one hour time limit. It will be Drapp's first appearance here since last fall.

. . .

Credits:
1) San Antonio Express, July 19, 1953
2) San Antonio Evening News, July 31, 1953
3) San Antonio Evening News, Aug. 21, 1953

8
Losing Battles

In the ring, and in the box office, the opposition did well on the first trip around their new circuit. In San Antonio, Bob Kline's first show at the Municipal Auditorium, with Nature Boy vs. Elephant Boy on top, drew 3,165 fans, according to research by Don Luce. The *San Antonio News* on May 5, reported 1,839 fans paying $1,619 for the second show, headlined by Elephant Boy beating Jack Kennedy and Nature Boy beating Jack O'Brien by disqualification. The challenge by Davis to Kennedy spiked the attendance to 2,500 on May 12, according to Luce. May 25, Kline moved to San Piedro Park and the next day the news reported "paid admissions totaled only 1,057 as a result of the switch from the Municipal Auditorium. Receipts came to $929.75." In the ring, Davis jumped O'Brien again. It led to a mixed tag where Jack O'Brien and Diamond Jim beat Davis and Farmer Pete, who subbed for no-show Sonny Boy Cassidy. According to the June 2 edition of the *Light*, 970 fans attended, "smallest crowd to attend a Kline mat show" with $954 total and net of $770.84.

In Corpus Christi, the opposition opened with promoter Jack Irwin running the Casino Arena, at the corner of Lexington Road at Weber. Tuesday, April, 26, the first show featured Elephant Boy against Johnny Dobbs. Barney Myers, the established promoter, ran his normal Thursday show at Town Hall on April 28, featuring Rito Romero against George Bollas on top. "Record Crowd of 2,500 Sees 'Wrestling War' at Casino" read the April 29 edition of the *Corpus Christi Caller-Times*.

"The 'wrestling war' came to town last night and before the Casino Arena show ended just about everything had happened. A record crowd, estimated by police as between 2,200 and 2,500 saw the show and about 300 got tired of bucking a late line of ticket buyers and went back home." The article mentioned the usual announcer did not show up for work that night and touched on the circumstances of the war in Corpus Christi, before detailing Irwin's plan to prepare better for the future. "We just didn't figure on the last minute rush for tickets," Irwin said in the story. "And next Tuesday we will make better arrangements for the handling of the crowd, no matter how late they come."

Unlike in San Antonio, the crowds did not wane. A *Times* column "Good Evening" by Joe Scherrer on June 29, headlined "5,000 See Mat Shows in One Week" detailed what he called a double record: "One week ago tomorrow night, 3,500 fans paid to see a wrestling show at the Casino Arena. The previous night, 1,500 bought tickets for Town Hall matches. The Casino crowd is regarded as the record for any wrestling show in Corpus Christi. The Town Hall crowd was a record for that arena. No one, not even Promoter Jack Irwin knows whether the next Casino card tomorrow night will draw another 3,500 crowd. And Barney Myers couldn't guess whether his show next Thursday night will attract another 1,500. What Wrestling War Casualties! About two months ago, the 'Texas wrestling war' spread to Corpus Christi when Promoter Irwin opened the Casino with wrestlers from the McLemore syndicate. Myers, a fixture in mat promotion here, continued business in the same old stand with Seigel (sic) wrestlers. The war broke out when (Sigel) and McLemore fell out. When wrestling competition came to town, with rival promoters staging a show each week, the wise men who were supposed to know about such things, were sure that the wrestling war would mean only one casualty — either Myers or Irwin. Their argument, which seemed to make sense, was that the town was not big enough to support two wrestling shows a week and that one of the promoters would have to fold. So what happens? In one week, 5,000 cash customers flock to the two wrestling arenas. That doesn't look like Irwin or Myers will be on a casualty list very soon."

In the June 1, 1953, NWA bulletin, Muchnick wrote he has been asked if St. Louis and Houston had a deal. "Yes, a deal does exist between St. Louis and Houston. It is a deal that exists between all Alliance members. While we aren't trying to cause trouble and start fights, but if they do start, we will be loyal to our members. I learned ... that the McLemore-McElyea combination would not be so confident, if they were not receiving comfort from some of our members. You know, in military circles, during times of war, it is treason to give aid and comfort to the enemy."

In Dallas that month, McLemore broke ground on the new Sportatorium. From a photo in the *Dallas News* on June 25: "Symbolizing the start of construction on a new Sportatorium. Promoter Ed McLemore, left, digs a spadeful of earth at the Cadiz and Industrial site. He gets an assist from a friend, Promoter Jack Pfefer of New York City. The old Sportatorium burned down May 1. The new one, costing $150,000 and seating 6,400, will house its first wrestling show in early September."

The ground breaking was a high point for the McLemore crew, but the pendulum swung back quickly. By the end of the month, Fort Worth promoter R.G. McElyea had switched sides, offended by McLemore's partner from New York. Tim Hornbaker documented the switch via the NWA's consent decree. By then, McElyea had sold his promotional interests in Fort Worth, and he spoke seemingly freely to the FBI during their investigation. (The FBI apparently had high hopes for McLemore's testimony, too, unaware he was back in the NWA by then. McLemore apparently gave the FBI basically nothing.) According to Hornbaker's reporting: "McElyea talked about the wrestling war between Ed McLemore and Morris Sigel, and said that Pfefer had come into Dallas to help McLemore with talent. According to the report, 'McElyea said that Pfefer was one of the loudest, vulgarest, and most objectionable men he had ever met. He said that McLemore and Pfefer came into his office, and Pfefer immediately said that he, McElyea, would have to get rid of certain wrestlers he then had working for him and that Pfefer would take care of supplying the talent. He said that

Mat Mogul Loses Promoters In Fort Worth, Wichita Falls

DALLAS, July 11 (AP)—Promoter Ed McLemore, who is waging a wrestling war against the combine operated by Morris Siegel of Houston, lost affiliated promoters in Fort Worth and Wichita Falls today.

That left McLemore with promotional tieups in five cities: Dallas, San Antonio, Corpus Christi, Waco and Mineral Wells.

It was reported that the Fort Worth and Wichita Falls promoters were joining the Siegel group, but McLemore said he had no information on that.

ROSE BOWL PROFITABLE

MADISON, Wis., July 11—UP—The University of Wisconsin made $41,585 from the 1953 Rose Bowl game, a report to the school's board of regents showed Saturday. The Pacific Coast and Western conferences split a net gate of $709,747, the report said.

Gals Steal Show At Auditorium

Rassling took a back seat at Municipal Auditorium Friday night as the gals staged a bang-up, slapstick comedy that put the paying customers in the aisle. Zuma's gyrations were overshadowed even though he won over Jack O'Brien with a fall and a disqualification in the main event.

The ladies did everything in the book and got away with it as the referee gaped and moaned.

The Slave Girl Moolah-Mars Bennett team, despite hair-pulling, slapping, kicking and punching, lost to the Princess Maritza-Daisy Mae-Darling Dagmar team in a tag-team match.

In the second main event Moolah won over the Princess.

In the top event Zuma won the legitimate fall with his favorite hold, the flying head scissors.

Newcomer Pedro Martinez tamed Johnny Shaw in 11 minutes, 20 seconds with a judo cut on the Adam's apple and a body press.

In the first preliminary Mars Bennett tripped Darling Dagmar

Credits:
1) Associated Press, July 11, 1953
2) San Antonio Evening News, Aug. 23, 1953
3) 1953 ad for Pappy's Showland matches promoted by Norman Clark

Pfefer, in effect, told him, McElyea, to stay out of the dressing room; that he, Pfefer, would run matters there while McElyea took care of selling tickets. McElyea said that this made him so mad that he decided to pull out right then.'"

McElyea wasn't the only one. The same July 11 Associated Press story that announced the switch in Fort Worth noted the promoter in Wichita Falls was switching sides, too. "That left McLemore with promotional tie-ups in five cities: Dallas, San Antonio, Corpus Christi, Waco and Mineral Wells. It was reported that the Fort Worth and Wichita Falls promoters were joining the Siegel (sic) group, but McLemore said he had no information on that."

By the end of the month, McLemore had lost his promoter in San Antonio, too. With the promotion fading from its strong start, and with entrenched opposition from the Livengood-Brown team at the Wrestlethon, Bob Kline decided to stop promoting after three months. According to news reports, he received $1,000 from the Texas Wrestling Agency to step aside.

From Scherrer's *Corpus Christi Caller-Times* column July 22, headlined, and still misspelled, "Siegel Sends Cash To Wrestling Way": "The two-month 'armistice' is over and the wrestling war has broken out along many Texas fronts as Morris (Sigel) turns loose his most potent weapon — hard cash — at Ed McLemore, his former partner. (Sigel), the mat mogul from Houston, and McLemore, from Dallas, split last February (sic) to kill a monopoly on the $2 million mat racket in the state. McLemore formed the Southwest Wrestling Agency to buck (Sigel's) Texas Wrestling Agency. McLemore's man here is Jack Irwin who opened the Casino Arena several months ago. (Sigel's) local man is Barney Myers who has been promoting wrestling bouts at Town Hall for 16 years. Jack and Barney have been stacking them in for weeks, and the mat war that ran hot during May and June seemed headed for a permanent deep freeze. Then, (Sigel) struck last week. He bought out McLemore's San Antonio promoter. He took over McLemore's top referee. He had a hand in the fold up of McLemore's promotions in Fort Worth and Wichita Falls."

The article indicated Irwin was also offered money. "They tried to buy me out for $1,000," he said in the article. "That was just a feeler. I told them I wasn't interested. I'm not interested, so they don't need to up any ante. I'm not quitter. I started with Ed McLemore, and I'm going to finish with Ed. If anyone doesn't think so, he doesn't know Jack Irwin."

In a section of the column with the subhead, "Too Much Irish In My Dad," Scherrer wrote about his call to the Dallas office, where instead of speaking with Ed, he got 21-year-old daughter Jeannie, who said she was authorized to speak for her father. "I can talk for Dad about Mr. Kline selling out to Mr. (Sigel) in San Antonio," she said. "No, I don't know how much was paid. No, sir, I wouldn't know why Mr. Kline would sell out. I only know that none of Dad's wrestlers have quit on him. I think that they want my father to quit. But there's too much Irish and German in my Dad, and he won't quit. He always has liked a fight and he will keep on fighting."

The column continued to document the recent side switching by Voss, and by the other promoters in Fort Worth and Wichita Falls. It said Sidney Balkin, a Sigel nephew, had bought Kline's promotion. It also noted McElyea was selling

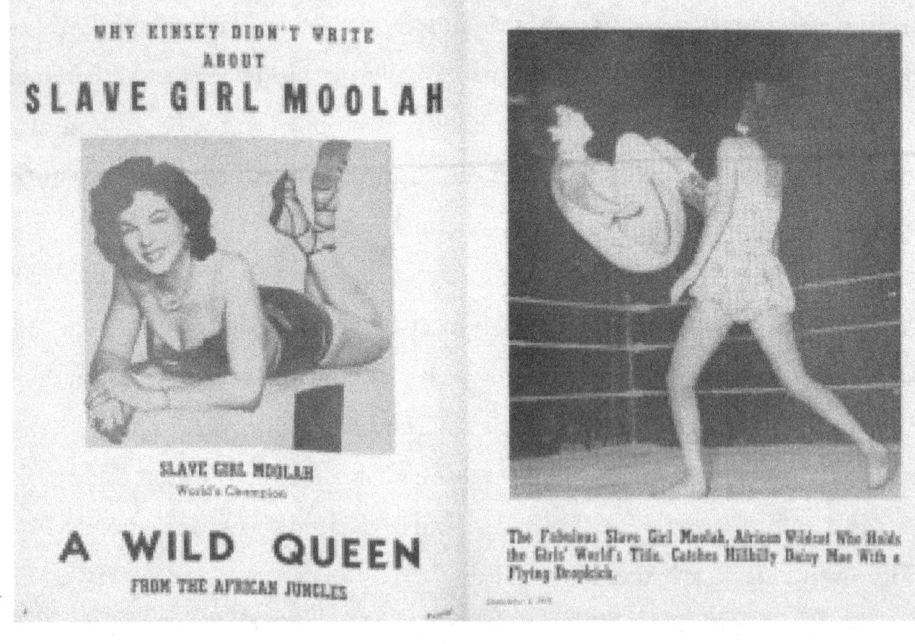

RASSLIN'

EVERY FRIDAY

Air Conditioned Municipal Auditorium

Bill Lawlor, Promoter Willard Brown, Matchmaker

JULY 31 San Antonio, Texas 10c

With Princess Maritza

NEW

WORLD'S CHAMPION

THE AMAZING

SOUTH AMERICAN

ZUMA

Who defeated Mr. America

In the Ring and Won the

Eastern World's Title

and Championship Belt

Credits:

1) July 31, 1953, San Antonio program announcing new champion. Courtesy of the Rare Books and Special Collections Department, Hesburgh Libraries, University of Notre Dame

his promotion to his son-in-law.

"All we know about that is that Mr. McElyea said he sold his stock to his son-in-law, Tim Moore, and that Mr. Moore rejoined Mr. (Sigel)," said Jeannie McLemore in the article.

It wasn't all bad for McLemore. In the summer, he brought in Pfefer's female troupe, headlined by Slave Girl Moolah. Roy Dunn was replaced by "Eastern World Champion" Argentina Zuma, an Argentina Rocca rip off who became popular, and the belt passed from Zuma to Tommy Phelps to Pedro Martinez. The cities that stayed on the Southwest circuit had their share of action.

In late summer, McLemore prepared his crowd for the Sportatorium's comeback. The last Fair Park show was Sept. 15, and featured Zuma and Martinez beating Leopard Boy and Jack O'Brien.

The next week the "Million Dollar Sportatorium" opened, with Nature Boy, as a surprise challenger to Zuma, taking the title. Phelps was a substitute for "Mr. America" Gene Stanlee, who did appear to set up the Sportatorium return Sept. 29. Moolah and the Lady Angel fought in the semi-main. Stanislaus Zbyszko appeared and accepted an award from McLemore. While he was in town, he made sure to tell a local newspaper columnist about his disdain for the current wrestlers. March of Dimes CEO Arthur Dyer made a presentation to thank McLemore for the annual donation from his anniversary show, a donation that was always five figures. Patients from the Scottish Rite Crippled Children's Hospital also thanked the promotion.

At Pappy's Showland on the 22nd, Duke Keomuka beat Bull Curry in a fight to the finish that ended after six falls when Curry could not continue. The next week featured an eight-man tag.

That same week, Keomuka and Ray Gunkel filed $9,000 damage suits against McLemore in a federal court in Dallas. According to the Associated Press on Sept. 24: "The wrestlers claim that they are entitled to $5 for each re-telecast of Dallas matches in which they appeared under terms of a contract they signed with McLemore in March of 1952. In their petitions, Keomuka and Gunkel said their matches had been re-televised all over the nation. They said they couldn't be certain as to just how many times the films of their matches had been televised, but estimated the number at 1,800 each. Beside asking damages, the wrestlers asked the court to restrain McLemore from further display of wrestling films in which they appear. Keomuka filed his suit under his real name of Martin Tanaka. He said his home was Los Angeles. Gunkel is from Chicago."

In November, rumors began to spread about the war ending. Again, Joe Scherrer, the Corpus Christi sport editor, captured the vibe of the McLemore side, beginning the Nov. 24 column with a subhead "McLemore Says 'No Truce Now'" and continued: "The wrestling war's cold as a blue norther, but there's no chance for an armistice 'right now.' You can take that for sure from Ed McLe-

GOOD EVENING

5,000 See Mat Shows In One Week

One week ago tomorrow night, 3,500 fans paid to see a wrestling show at the Casino Arena. The previous night, 1,500 bought tickets for Town Hall matches.

The Casino crowd is regarded as the record for any wrestling show in Corpus Christi. The Town Hall crowd was a record for that arena. No one not even Promoter Jack Irwin knows whether the Casino card tomorrow night will draw another 3,500 crowd. And Barney Myers couldn't guess whether his show next Thursday night will attract another 1,500.

What Wrestling War Casualties!!

About two months ago, the "Texas wrestling war" spread to Corpus Christi when Promoter Irwin opened the Casino with wrestlers from the McLemore syndicate. Myers, a fixture in mat promotion here, continued business in the same old stand with Seigel wrestlers. The war broke out when Seigel and McLemore fell out.

When wrestling competition came to town, with rival promoters staging a show each week, the wise men who were supposed to know about such things, were sure that the wrestling war would mean only one casualty — either Myers or Irwin. Their argument, which seemed to make sense, was that the town was not big enough to support two wrestling shows a week and that one of the promoters would have to fold.

So what happens? In one week, 5,000 cash customers flock to the two wrestling arenas. That doesn't look like either Irwin or Myers will be on a casualty list very soon.

GOOD EVENING

What Do You Mean Wrestling War?

[illegible]

GOOD EVENING

Siegel Sends Cash To Wrestling Way

[illegible]

Irwin Turns Down $1,000 Offer

[illegible]

'Too Much Irish In My Dad'

[illegible]

Leo Voss Goes Back To Siegel

[illegible]

Credits: 1953 Corpus Christi Times columns by Joe Scherrer, June 29, July 22, Sept. 23

more, who's been feuding since last February with Morris Sigel over the million-dollar-a-year wrestling take in Texas. You can also take that for sure from Karl (Doc) Sarpolis, who's just teamed up with McLemore as a partner in supplying wrestling talent to promoters in Texas and Oklahoma." Scherrer got the scoop when McLemore and Sarpolis were in town Wednesday, Nov. 18, to see a main event of Tommy Phelps and Leopard Boy vs. Pedro Martinez and Mexican Joe. They were also there to talk shop with Irwin.

Everyone was in denial mode about a settlement. Under the subhead "Wrestling Profits Whittled" the details followed. "'I had a talk with Sigel some time ago ... but I tell you there's no chance now for an armistice, as you call it.' Up popped Sarpolis: 'There's no chance so far as I am concerned. I quit Sigel because I didn't like the methods he used to try to keep Ed out of business.' Has the wrestling war — hot and cold — dipped into the Sigel and McLemore profits? 'Naturally, that's so,' said McLemore, "the same as it would be if any other business monopoly had been split into two competing businesses.' How much has McLemore lost since the split? 'I don't think that's a fair question,' said McLemore, 'but I'll say that whatever we've lost, it's not enough to get us out of the business. I don't mean lost. I mean our profits were cut. And so were Sigel's, I guess. That's for him to say.'" The next section, with subhead "Jack Irwin Wouldn't Sell Out" began with a shocker. "McLemore was frank to admit that at one stage of the feud Sigel had him on the ropes. 'Yes, sir, you're right,' he said. 'He (Sigel) bought out all of our promoters except Jack Irwin. I don't know how much he paid them. But we've overcome that, and now we're providing wrestlers for 10 towns. Sigel's got about the same number of towns, but we're still going to grow.'"

And then, ironically: "McLemore and Sarpolis seemed to fret more about unlimited television of wrestling shows cutting into their profits than to fret about Sigel's opposition. 'Sure,' said McLemore, 'we made some money by televising our shows. But it begins to look like there's going to be too much TV. You know on some stations there's as much as 10 hours of televised wrestling.

WE DEFY AND CHALLENGE

Any and all crooks connected with the Wrestling Business

All fake champions, their stooges and stool pigeons with strong arm methods

We hate big Stalins and Little Stalins Big Hitlers and Little Hitlers

We hate Despots Who are Mad crazy for power

We love freedom and free enterprize and Free Competition

We defy and challenge Un-American Methods of Black Listng and Threats

We Challenge Shady Deals Behind Closed Doors

WE SAY HANDS OFF THE GREAT ANCIENT SPORT OF WRESTLING

THIS IS AMERICA GOD BLESS OUR FREE COUNTRY

ATTENTION TO OUR PATRONS

We suggest you read **TRUE MAGAZINE**, August Issue, the expose of wrestling racketeers and crooks who infested the sport, by the venerable Stanley Zbyszko, Dean of American Wrestlers and recognized as the greatest wrestler who ever lived. Read this interesting expose of morons and human parasites.

2

Credits:

1) Aug. 14, 1953 San Antonio program after Morris Sigel bought out Ed McLemore's first promoter in San Antonio.
Courtesy of the Rare Books and Special Collections Department, Hesburgh Libraries, University of Notre Dame

Well, about three hours would be best for us. When you get more than that, and when you get competing TV show, your gate's bound to be hurt."

The column goes on to focus on Sarpolis, his football days, his matches with Ed "Strangler" Lewis, and his concepts of featuring lighter weight wrestlers, the kind the NWA does not want to use, he said. The column ended with a section about the two men's grandchildren. It is an interesting look at the year from the Dallas perspective.

However, the Corpus Christi situation seems to be the outlier. On different nights, with obviously different crews and storylines, both promoters were having success. In San Antonio, that was not the case. McLemore's brother-in-law, Bill Lawlor, was struggling against the Livengood-Brown team.

Dallas was still a draw at best. Although it was not successful, McLemore did return to twice a week Dallas shows in the fall, trying to run the Sportatorium on Friday nights in November and December of 1953.

The McLemore crew never got to Houston. Dizzy Davis headlined in Los Angeles and in Leroy McGuirk's towns, as well as Wichita Falls in the fall of 1953, but his only appearances in Houston were when he went home to Almeda.

However, Southwest did set up its own Texas circuit and run it successfully enough to set a precedent for future decades, when it would finally take over the Texas booking office.

A year into the war, nothing had been settled. Both sides had suffered. And yet, business as a whole had been good in the state of Texas. The *Houston Chronicle* and Associated Press reported the state receipts totaled $1.761 million in ticket sales from September 1952 to September 1953, with $47,862.80 collected in taxes on those sales. The AP reported 43 towns had matches during the year, with 31 being weekly or regular towns, although five or 10 were wrestling war double shots. The *Chronicle* reported Sigel "guided the spot in Houston to its biggest box office year" and as one of the few cities unmarked by the war, it made sense.

In Dallas, which had been the biggest drawing city in the state two years earlier, the crowds were down, and split. “In 1951, Dallas was the state’s top wrestling town. Ed McLemore, who was the only promoter in Dallas then, said a good year for him was ‘a quarter of a million.’ And a bad year? ‘There were no bad years,’ he said.” He said he left the NWA because their principles no longer aligned. “McLemore now puts on two wrestling shows a week at his Sportatorium and the Texas Wrestling Alliance promotes once a week at Pappy’s Showland. McLemore admits he is not making money. He says that the scrap is hurting the business and that neither side is making money in Dallas. The opposition says it is making money. There is too much wrestling in the Dallas-Fort Worth area with rival promotions. Five nights of the week you can see wrestling live or on TV in Dallas. The wrestling agency and McLemore both hold shows on Tuesday. Both shows are televised. McLemore’s other show is on Friday.”

Norman Clark said he was making money in Dallas. “I’m in no wrestling war,” he said. “I don’t worry about the other guy. I just put on my matches. That’s absolutely true. We made money in 1953. We met our expenses, plus the lawyer’s fees, court fees and then made money.”

Clark defended the Alliance system and the boys’ need to keep working with Alliance promoters. He again downplayed the rivalry. “We run 75 percent of capacity. If he closed tomorrow we could do only 25 percent more business. I’m optimistic. I think it will be the best year we’ve had.”

McLemore is quoted at the end, reiterating his desire to extend the war, and to expand it to Houston and Fort Worth. “I guess I’m just a stubborn Irishman. I’m gonna fight it to the end.”

The column concludes: “There is one thing you can bank on, wrestling, like chili, is in Texas to stay. A business that makes a million dollars a year is bound to be popular with some people. If the fan can stand it, he’ll get lots of wrestling in 1954.”

9
The End

NWA President Sam Muchnick had a lot of problems as 1954 began. The NWA started in 1948 with six Midwestern promotions. Their goals were mostly about protecting the business and they were, for a brief moment, unified in their vision. By 1954, Muchnick had been president for four years. The NWA had swelled to nearly 30 members and there was no unity. There was Muchnick, herding cats. In 1953, there had been territory wars in Texas and Southern California, there were conflicts between founder Pinkie George and other promoters, and the seeds were being planted for the anti-trust lawsuit and FBI investigation of wrestling.

According to Tim Hornbaker, at basically the same time the FBI began poking around NWA business to see if the rumors about industry blackballing were true, Houston promoter and TWA owner Morris Sigel was submitting names to Muchnick of wrestlers who were going against the NWA faction in Texas. Among the names Sigel reportedly tried to blackball were Antone Leonne in March 1954, and Tarzan White and Al Massey in April 1954. Among the notes FBI agent Roy Disney made in his files was his observation that Muchnick had cooperated, and seemed to be an honest man, and since so much incriminating evidence was found in his files, Muchnick probably wasn't hiding or destroying evidence.

By 1956, Muchnick, Sigel and the other NWA members would be signing a consent decree acknowledging their illegal practices and vowing to do better or be disbanded.

McLEMORE, SIGEL END DALLAS WRESTLING WAR

Dallas' 17-month-old wrestling war ended officially Saturday, although two mat cards will be presented here for one more week.

Ed McLemore Jr., Dallas promoter, and Morris Sigel, Houston promoter and head of the Texas booking office of the National Wrestling Alliance, Saturday agreed to resume a partnership under which they promoted at the Sportatorium for thirteen years—prior to January, 1953.

At that time, McLemore and Sigel split in a dispute over film television receipts. McLemore continued to promote at the Sportatorium, but Sigel and his associates, Frank Burke and Norman Clark, moved to Dallas and promoted rival mat shows at Pappy's Showland.

Under resumption of the partnership, McLemore, Sigel and Burke will stage their first show, June 1. All future Dallas matches will be at the Sportatorium.

McLemore, who returned to Dallas Saturday night, after completing arrangements with Sigel in Houston, said the agreement represented a "compromise."

"It was a mutual agreement," McLemore said. "The misunderstanding which disrupted our partnership has been resolved."

Two Dallas television stations—WFAA-TV, Channel 8, and KRLD-TV, Channel 4, will carry live telecasts of the Tuesday night cards, simultaneously, probably through September. Definite television commitments have not been made past that time.

Several other points were settled, McLemore said. He said he would work with the Alliance in handling any future wrestling film for television and would not stage any rival promotions. Besides Dallas, Corpus Christi is the only city in which two shows have been held weekly. McLemore will discontinue his promotion there.

Sigel has promoted in Fort Worth, Waco, San Antonio, Houston, Corpus Christi and Galveston, and will continue to do so.

McLemore's other promotions have included Marshall, Tyler, Laredo and Del Rio. Some of these may be continued, McLemore said, since none are in competing cities or areas.

The bulk of the wrestlers, who will appear on future Sportatorium cards, will be NWA members, McLemore said.

"As usual, I will have the pick of the alliance wrestlers, but I probably will keep some of the others who have been working with me in recent months. I'll have a free hand in that respect."

The compromise came at a time when both Dallas mat promotions were suffering at the gate. Neither approached the crowds which once made Dallas one of the nation's best wrestling cities.

McLemore, unable to use alliance wrestlers, had to line-up his own.

His difficulties were compounded when the Sportatorium burned and he was forced to move his show to Fair Park Livestock Pavillion until a new building could be erected.

The new Sportatorium has a slightly smaller seating capacity than the old building but still can handle approximately 5,500 fans.

So, in the spring of 1954, Muchnick got involved in the Texas Rasslin' War. Although the rumors of an end to the war had been reported since November, according to later reports, the NWA arranged negotiations — some say forced — which began in March.

While that was going on, the war continued in Dallas, Corpus Christi, San Antonio and a few smaller towns. Sonny Myers and Cyclone Anaya freshened up the top of the cards on the TWA circuit, with Myers being billed as returning after a 15-month absence.

Jan. 26, the day of McLemore's big anniversary show, the opposition countered with Sonny Myers and Sugi Sito beating Don Evans and Danny Savich. Danny McShain beat Cyclone Anaya, Timothy Geohagen beat Danno O'Shocker, Dick Hutton beat Bob Cummings, Larry Hamilton beat Ramon Zavalza and Willie Love beat Bud Richardson. Savich also won a 12-man, $500 battle royal.

At the Sportatorium, McLemore ran his 16th anniversary show with the March of Dimes. Suddenly, briefly, Roy Dunn returned as world heavyweight champion, beating Mexican Joe in the main event. Ted Cox Sr. and Ted Cox Jr. and Super Swedish Angel topped some cards, but the core of Nature Boy Tommy Phelps, Elephant Boy, Pedro Martinez, Jack Kennedy and Jack O'Brien continued to mix into cards, up and down the weekly lineups.

Leone made his Sportatorium debut March 30, beating Mexican Joe in a semi-main event. At Pappy's that night, Duke Keomuka beat Bull Curry by disqualification in the main event, but something more interesting happened on the undercard. Love beat Richardson again, in a match between two Black wrestlers. However, Love was a late substitute for Emerson Cozier Jr. Sometimes billed as Emerson Crozier, he was scheduled to wrestle, but instead was arrested. From the *Dallas Morning News* on April 1, headlined "Loses Fall, Wrestler Listed as Being AWOL": "A wrestler scheduled to appear in a Dallas grunt and groan arena Tuesday night found himself grappling with the Federal Bureau of Investigation instead. He lost. In fact, he never even got to the arena. Nabbed at the door as he left the house in the 1906 block of Boll where he had been staying was Emerson Cozier Jr. According to Special Agent J.K. Mumford, Cozier deserted Fort Hood in December 1953." The short article ends by saying Cozier also lost the second fall, "when the FBI turned him over to military police on Wednesday." Not much is known about Cozier, and there is no follow up in the papers about his arrest. However, there are some match listings for him in the later 1950s. It is possible he did some jail time and returned to the wrestling circuit. However, the greater mystery is if his arrest had anything to do with the wrestling war. The answer to that is as well known as the identity of Tony from Houston. In any event, the availability of Love as a substitute meant the matches were not harmed greatly. Richardson was often billed as the champion of the Black wrestlers and Love was arguably more well known and popular than Cozier, so the show went on.

However, it was clear the stress of the war was affecting everybody. Clark had a heart attack in the spring. Sigel resigned as chair of the NWA television committee, citing his own health issues. With Sarpolis gone and his partner ailing, the task of running the circuit went to Frank Burke, who now had to get more involved in Dallas, as well. At some point, Sarpolis left Texas for California, where he applied for NWA membership in partnership with an outlaw effort by Johnny Doyle to take Los Angeles from the Eatons. He did not get NWA membership in California.

In San Antonio, Bill Lawlor's cards seemed to be getting stale. Thursday, Feb. 18, Phil Sylva headlined in a handicap match, beating Ellis Bashara and the Golden Terror. Wrestlingdata.com lists the attendance as 293 people. The Wrestlethon show the night before, headlined by Stu Gibson beating Prince Maiava, drew 2,117, according to the same website. Thursday, Feb. 25, according to the *San Antonio News*, Lawlor featured a match of college grapplers, Frank Kapral from Michigan State and Bill Vohaska from Illinois. The Cox father and son team took on Martinez and Mexican Joe in the semi-main. The night before at the Wrestlethon, Antonio Rocca beat Stu Gibson in the main event, with Duke

New Villains Test Mat Heroes

Two brand spanking new villains, neither of whom has appeared in San Antonio previously, will test the latest mat heroes Friday night when Bill Lawlor takes his pro wrestling carnival back to the Municipal Auditorium.

Leoprad Boy, a fearsome bearded culprit, will attempt to end the victory streak of Argentina Zuma, the acrobatic South American who has won five straight bouts here.

Goliath, a seven foot, seven-inch monster who tips the Fairbanks at 275 pounds, collides with Pedro Martinez in another feature attraction.

Zuma and Martinez will team up to take on Nature Boy and Jack O'Brien in a tag team match that promises plenty of fireworks.

In the other bouts O'Brien meets Baron George Grant and Nature Boy meets Bill Powell, erstwhile referee, in the curtain raiser. The first bout goes on at 8:30 p.m.

WRESTLETHON

Gloria Barattini, the wealthy girl who gave up a singing career for wrestling, will be a featured performer on next Wednesday night's mat program at the Wrestlethon Arena, Matchmaker Frank Brown announced Friday.

She will be paired against Mae Young, the drop kick star, in a one-fall match that will be wrestled to a finish.

The main event and other bouts will be announced Sunday, Brown said.

Wrestlers Sue Dallas Promoter

DALLAS, Sept. 24—(AP)—Two Dallas wrestlers, Duke Keomuka and Ray Gunkel, have filed $9000 damage suits against Promoter Ed McLemore jr. of Dallas in Federal District court.

The wrestlers claim that they are entitled to $5 for each retelecast of Dallas matches in which they appeared under terms of a contract which they signed with McLemore in March of 1952.

In their petitions Keomuka and Gunkel said their matches had been retelevised all over the nation. They said they couldn't be certain as to just how many times the films of their matches had been televised, but estimated the number at 1800 each.

Besides asking damages, the wrestlers asked the court to restrain McLemore from further display of wrestling films in which they appear.

Keomuka filed his suit under his real name of Martin Tanaka. He said his home was Los Angeles. Gunkel is from Chicago.

Credits:

1) San Antonio Evening News, Sept. 4, 1953

2) San Antonio Light, Sept. 24, 1953

WED., MAR. 10 at 8:30 LEXINGTON BLVD. WEBER ROAD

FROM EUROPE
SWEDISH
Angel
WORLD'S UGLIEST MAN WRESTLER
330 POUNDS

FIRST APPEARANCE HERE FOR THIS INTERNATIONALLY KNOWN DEMON OF WRESTLING!!

VS:

Golden Terror
310 LBS. OF BEEF
GOLDEN, COLO. MEANIE

Pedro Martinez — 90 MINUTES Vs. 2 OF 3 FALLS — King Kong Cox

FARMER ANDREWS — TAG — ELEPHANT BOY
MEXICAN JOE — TEAM — NATURE BOY

3 OTHER FAST EXCITING PRELIMINARIES

ADVANCE SALE OF TICKETS: CALL 4-5414

RINGSIDE 1.50 — RES. 1.00 — 1000 Seats at 50c — PROMOTER — JACK IRWIN

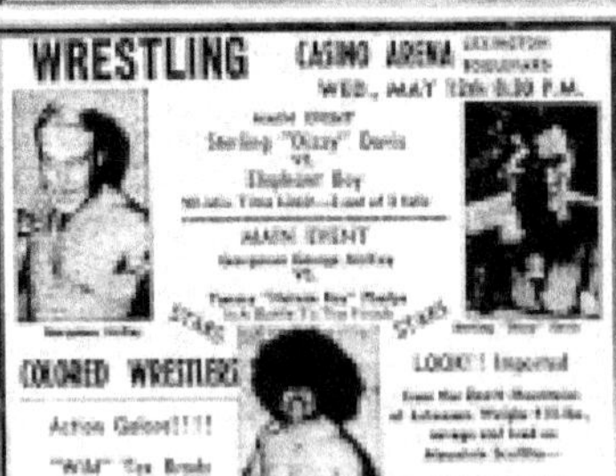

College Stars On Mat Card

Two main events, one matching a pair of former college grappling stars and the other bringing together four rugged veterans in a tag team affair, is top Promoter Bill Lawlor's wrestling card at the Municipal Auditorium Thursday night. The program begins at 8:15 p.m.

Frank Kapral, former Michigan State All-American guard and a Big Ten wrestling king, takes on Bill Vohaska, ex-Illinois wrestling and football ace, in what shapes up as a scientific affair.

The tag team event finds King Kong Cox and his son, Ted, Jr., going against the Latin-American twosome of Pedro Martinez and Mexican Joe.

Both main events are for two out of three falls with a one hour time limit.

Four one fall matches also are slated. They are Philip Sylva vs Elephant Boy; Kanae vs Frank Marlowe, King Kong Cox vs Mexican Joe, and King Kong, Jr., vs Pedro Martinez.

Credits:

1) Ads for Jack Irwin shows in Corpus Christi, March 9, May 5 & May 11, 1954

2) SanAntonio Express , Feb. 25, 1954

Keomuka beating Larry Hamilton in the semi-main, with Anaya, Myers and Angelo Savoldi on the card. Wrestlingdata.com lists the attendance at the Wrestlethon as 1,879 and the attendance the next day for an hour Broadway between the college stars as 334.

The Feb. 25 show ended Lawlor's run in San Antonio. The Livengood-Brown team continued to draw about 2,000 fans weekly in March. The established promoters with their own building did not just survive the war, they won. They would continue in business for decades.

In Corpus Christi, the split decision produced the most controversial ending. Business continued to do well at the established Town Hall for Barney Myers, but Jack Irwin's shows at the Casino Arena also continued to succeed. In March, Town Hall had main events featuring a round-robin of action between Gibson, Keomuka and Maiava, as well as a March 4, main event for the Texas title with Ray Gunkel defending against Cyclone Anaya.

Lou Thesz toured Texas twice in the spring, bringing the NWA World Heavyweight title to the TWA towns and West Texas, too. In April, Thesz wrestled Stu Gibson in San Antonio on Wednesday the 14th; Bull Curry in Galveston on Thursday the 15th; Prince Maiava in Houston on Friday the 16th; Don Evans in Dallas on Tuesday the 20th; and Dory Funk in Amarillo on Thursday the 22nd. It is possible he worked some spot shows that week, too. In May, he wrestled Evans in Fort Worth on Monday the 10th; Ray Gunkel in Austin on Tuesday the 11th; and Gibson in San Antonio on Wednesday the 12th. A week later, after a couple of matches in Mexico against Gori Guerrero, Thesz returned. He wrestled Wilbur Snyder in El Paso on Tuesday the 25th; and Black Guzman in Houston on Friday the 28th. Thesz was scheduled to wrestle Rito Romero in Victoria on Wednesday the 26th, but according to his title history, he missed that date.

While this was going on, Muchnick was apparently forcing a sit-down between McLemore and Sigel. "McLemore, Sigel end Dallas Wrestling War," read the *Dallas Morning News* on Sunday, May 23, 1954. The first sign of an end to the war was Keomuka appearing at the Sportatorium on Tuesday, May 25, to face Gorgeous George McKay, on a card otherwise filled with McLemore regulars. "Dallas' 17-month-old wrestling war officially ended Saturday, although two more mat cards will be presented for one more week. Ed McLemore Jr., Dallas promoter, and Morris Sigel, Houston promoter and head of the Texas booking office of the National Wrestling Alliance, Saturday agreed to resume a partnership under which they promoted at the Sportatorium for thirteen years — prior to January 1953. At that time, McLemore and Sigel split in a dispute over film television receipts. McLemore continued to promote at the Sportatorium, but Sigel and his associates, Frank Burke and Normal Clark, moved to Dallas and promoted rival mat shows at Pappy's Showland. Under resumption of the partnership, McLemore, Sigel and Burke will stage their first show June 1. All future Dallas matches will be at the Sportatorium."

The article reported McLemore had been in Houston for negotiations and he told the paper the settlement was "a compromise" and "the misunderstanding that disrupted our partnership has been resolved." Other reports indicate Muchnick also attended. In the agreement, Sigel and company gained 50 percent of the Dallas promotion and TV receipts. TWA shut down their Dallas shows, while McLemore agreed to shut down his only opposition town remaining, Corpus Christi. Sigel would continue to book to Fort Worth, Waco, San Antonio, Corpus Christi and Galveston, as well as his Houston home base. McLemore's promoters in Marshall, Tyler, Laredo and Del Rio could join the new group, since they were promoting their cities without opposition from the Sigel group.

The *Houston Press* reported May 22, 1954, that all of McLemore's promoters had gone bankrupt, except for Jack Irwin in Corpus Christi. The story quoted McLemore about the talent imbalance between the two groups. "It was like competing with the New York Yankees with a county fair ball club."

May 20, 1954, Sigel wired Muchnick: "Entire Dallas deal consummated in very satisfactory manner. Start booking in their territory immediately. Regards, Morris P. Sigel"

Thesz, Evans At Showland

Lou Thesz will risk his world's heavyweight wrestling crown at Pappy's Showland Tuesday night against Don Evans in the best-of-three-falls, 90-minute limit headliner of Promoter Norman Clark's five-bout card.

WFAA-TV, Channel 8, will telecast the first four bouts of the wrestling program direct from Pappy's Showland beginning at 8:30 p.m. Tuesday.

Duke Keomuka and Larry Chene, who wrestled to a draw last week, will be rematched in the best-of-three-falls, 45-minute-limit semifinal.

The one-fall, 20-minute-limit top preliminary will pair two old rivals, Rito Romero and Bull Curry.

Two other one-fall bouts will round out the card. One will pit Stu Gibson and Prince Maiava; newcomer Paddy Muldoon will tackle Alo Leilani in the 8:30 p.m. opener.

LOSES FALLS

Wrestler Listed as Being AWOL

A wrestler scheduled to appear in a Dallas grunt and groan arena Tuesday night found himself grappling with the Federal Bureau of Investigation instead.

He lost.

In fact, he never even got to the arena.

Nabbed at the door as he left the house in the 1900 block of Boll where he had been staying was Emerson Cozier Jr.

J. K (Jack) Mumford, special agent in charge of the Dallas office, said Cozier had been listed as a deserter from Fort Hood since December.

Cozier, who wrestled under the name of Emerson Crozier, lost the first fall with the FBI. Then he lost the second Wednesday when military policemen started back to Fort Hood with him in tow.

Credits:
1) Dallas Morning News, April 20, 1954
2) Dallas Morning News, April 1, 1954

McLemore said he would use NWA wrestlers again but he would also keep his top stars from the past year. He would continue to have final say in booking Dallas. "The compromise came at a time when both Dallas mat promotions were suffering at the gate. Neither approached the crowds which once made Dallas one of the nation's best wrestling cities," the *Dallas Morning News* article concluded.

There is no mention of Doc Sarpolis in the article, but he appears to leave the Dallas office for good at this time and did not return to the TWA fold. An article that year from *The Vindicator* reported Sarpolis bought a motel east of Houston in Dayton, Texas, The Valley Hotel Courts, and was also playing a lot of golf. His third of the Texas Wrestling Agency had already been bought out, and his two ninths of the Dallas office appeared to return to McLemore, who now owned half of Dallas rather than a third. Sigel and Burke got the other half of the Dallas office and their share of the television receipts.

Sigel explained his side of the dispute to Muchnick. "Doc says he admires my principles but not my methods," he wrote. "He's said that before. If he means by that when a guy is cutting my throat I'll fight him with everything in my power, he's right."

Sigel claimed McLemore never wanted to include Sarpolis in the partnership in TWA or Dallas. "Then in the very last part of 1952 and first part of 1953 came the blowup between Mac on one side and Doc, Frank and me on the other, and when Mac claimed in open court that Doc, Frank and me weren't his partners. Doc was just as burned up about this as I and he should remember that Russell Bonham was his attorney and mine also advised us that Frank and I should file a suit against Mac and Doc so it could be brought in Houston to get an accounting for all the moneys that had been held out on Frank and me and also partly on Doc."

"Mac came to Houston and told us that he was losing money and that he wanted to get together with Frank and me and form a corporation to promote wrestling in Dallas," Sigel continued, "with him owning half of the stock and

Frank and me the other half. Doc wasn't with Frank at that time and his name was never mentioned."

McLemore kept his town, lost the opposition and got the bigger name wrestlers back at the new Sportatorium. His popular wrestling show was going to upgrade its talent and the war did nothing to harm his music show, except when it forced a change in venue after the fire. The issue with the dried river bed had been resolved by the arson. The "new million dollar Sportatorium" became famous during the World Class Championship Wrestling era in the 1980s and continued to be the home of McLemore's two popular television shows, promoting the "grunt and groan" men and the "hill-billy" music.

McLemore later told the FBI he lost $80,000 during the war, but that figure does not seem to take into account the $100,000 portion of the Sportatorium rebuild the insurance did not cover. He said he thought Sigel lost a significant amount of money, too. Sigel always minimized his losses, saying they were mostly legal fees in the low five figures. He and Clark said the Pappy's shows were, at least, not money losers. Of course, by the end of the war, a town that had been doing four to six thousand fans weekly, and was often the top wrestling city in Texas, was averaging half of that, split between two or three shows.

In the match at the Sportatorium May 25, Keomuka beat Tommy Phelps. At the same time, Danny McShain was beating Rito Romero on the last card at Pappy's Showland. Tuesday, June 1, Romero got revenge as he and McShain moved their feud to the main event at the Sportatorium. Don Evans beat Paul Boesch, who was a substitute for Keomuka, prevented from wrestling for storyline reasons.

In his notes to the NWA members in summer 1954, Muchnick hailed the peace agreement: "Congratulations to Morris Sigel and Ed McLemore on the renewal of their business agreements. This office was kept informed by Morris Sigel on all negotiations for the past two months. Let's hope that the alignment again of Sigel and McLemore proves beneficial to Dallas and to Texas wrestling and to the Alliance."

Keomuka Returning to Sportatorium

Duke Keomuka will bring his famed judo back to the Sportatorium wrestling wars Tuesday night, meeting Gorgeous George McKay in a best of three falls, 60-minute limit bout that will feature the double main event program.

A two-out-of-three falls tag team match will serve as the cofeature. It pairs Irish Jack Kennedy and Tommy (Nature Boy) Phelps against Jack O'Brien and the hooded Golden Terror.

Sandwiched between the cofeatures is a one-fall-to-a-finish scrap between the 400-pound Ozark Giant and the Elephant Boy. Two weeks ago, the Ozark Giant won from the Elephant Boy taking two straight falls with a pair of bear hugs.

Three one-fall, 15-minute limit scraps round out the card. The opener will match Dick Bryant against Roy Kendall, while Phelps and the Golden Terror will meet in the second match. Chuck Benson will tackle Sammy Balwwin in the third event.

Wrestling War In Texas Ends

Effect Of McLemore-Sigel Merger Here Unknown

800 Seeking PGA Berths

Credits:
1) Dallas Morning News, May 23, 1954
2) Corpus Christi Caller, May 23, 1954

The same letter then mentioned Sigel's resignation as head of the Alliance's Television Committee, citing his health and how it has limited his ability to travel. Muchnick appointed Chicago promoter Leonard Schwartz to replace Sigel, who stayed on the committee, because, "this is one of the most important committees in the Alliance, and the President is calling upon all of its members to be working the problem, so that when we meet in September, we might be able to come up with some solution."

For a war that lasted nearly 18 months and encompassed two-thirds of Texas, it ended suddenly and with most of the loose ends tied up quickly.

Corpus Christi played out differently.

On May 23, the *Corpus Christi Caller-Times* had its own story, from Sports Editor Roy Terrell, with the headline "Wrestling War in Texas Ends" and a subhead "Effect of McLemore-Sigel Merger Here Unknown," which described the story through the local lens. "Corpus Christi is the only other city in which two shows have been held weekly. The Dallas story hinted that McLemore will discontinue his promotion here, but Sigel will continue. Jack Irwin, who has been promoting matches at the Casino Arena on Lexington Boulevard since last April with McLemore as his booking agent was completely puzzled when contacted yesterday. 'I don't know what it's all about,' he said. Irwin added that he had a wrestling card lined up for Wednesday night and that the show would definitely go on as scheduled. 'What happens after that, I don't know,' he said. 'You know as much about it as I do.' Barney Myers, the Town Hall Arena promoter and a longtime Sigel man, would only say 'there must be some basis of fact for all the rumors we've been hearing.'"

The article admitted that some facts about the end of the war were lacking but there were some things that could be drawn out from the rumors and facts available: "For one, it was apparent McLemore, reported to be losing money heavily, had decided to get back in with Sigel and his more powerful group. He will cease booking wrestling for his promoters around the state after this week. There were really few left running, anyway, with Corpus Christi apparently one of the strong spots. Both Irwin and Myers have been drawing consistently good crowds here, with the Casino holding shows on Wednesday nights and Town Hall on Thursdays. Other McLemore promoters haven't done so well. The split in Fort Worth lasted only a few short weeks and ceased in San Antonio about a month ago. There was never a rival promoter in Sigel's stronghold, Houston. Irwin didn't know yesterday whether he might be able to obtain wrestlers in the future from some other booking agency or not. 'I don't know a thing,' he repeated. 'And what I do know, I'm not telling yet. You will probably hear a lot more from me later this week.'"

Wednesday, May, 26, the *Corpus Christi Caller-Times* ran its Good Evening column from Joe Scherrer, with the initial subheadline, "Jack Irwin Learns The Hard Way" and an update on the aftermath in the city. "You've got to hand it to Jack Irwin, the Casino wrestling promoter. When he makes a deal he goes through with it, even to the bitter end. A little over a year ago, Irwin made a deal with Ed McLemore, the Dallas wrestling promoter. Irwin, an ex-boxer and fight manager, made a deal with McLemore to put on McLemore's wrestlers at the Casino Arena. When Irwin made the deal he didn't know anything about the angles in the wrestling game. He's wiser tonight, as he goes through on his end of a deal that McLemore called off last week. McLemore sent Irwin a brief wire that he would no longer furnish wrestlers for Jack's shows after tonight. Only a few short weeks before, Irwin and McLemore — the old deal still on — had made plans for bigger and better wrestling shows. Irwin hasn't been able to get McLemore on the telephone since he got the deal's-off wire. Jack did get through to one of McLemore's assistants, who seemed surprised that Irwin was going through with tonight's card."

Irwin made all seats cheap for the finale. "Throwing a 'Farewell' Party" read the subhead: "Why is Irwin offering his 'farewell' show at 50 cents a head? He could fill that big Casino Arena tonight, and the chances are he wouldn't make a dime. 'You can say,' said Jack, 'that when I make a deal I go through to the end. A lot of people tell me they have liked the shows I put on: so just say that I'm

LAST CASINO SHOW

Irwin Charges He Was 'Sold Down the River'

Conrad Lone Favorite Still In Southern

Irwin Files On Sigel

DALLAS — (AP) — Wrestling promoters Ed McLemore of Dallas and Morris Sigel and Frank Burke of Houston were named in a $208,721 anti-trust suit filed in federal court here Friday by Jack Irwin, Corpus Christi wrestling promoter.

Irving charged that McLemore, Sigel and Burke have attempted to "monopolize the wrestling business in Texas, being engaged in the business of promoting and booking professional wrestling." More specifically it alleged breach of contract.

The suit charged that Irwin entered into a contract in 1953 with McLemore to put on local shows in Corpus Christi, with wrestlers to be provided by McLemore. For this, the petition said, McLemore would receive 65 per cent of the receipts out of which he would pay the wrestlers, with 35 per cent to go to Irwin.

Irwin claimed he put on 54 shows under the contract at a cost of $19,570 and that on May 26, 1954, he was notified by McLemore that he could not be supplied with any more wrestlers.

Credits:
1) Corpus Christi Times, May 27, 1954
2) Houston Post, June 25, 1955

throwing a party for my last show under the deal that McLemore has called off.'"

The column ended with a reminder of McLemore and Doc Sarpolis visiting the city months earlier. "McLemore was asked: 'What's the chance of a truce with Sigel? And if there is a truce and only one show goes here, what happens to your man Jack Irwin?' McLemore said there weren't any signs of a truce — and that if one should be signed and there were only one show here, Irwin 'wouldn't go.'"

The next day, the *Corpus Christi Caller-Times* summed up the final show: "Irwin Charges He Was 'Sold Down River'" read the headline and also the first line of the article, quoting Irwin's intermission speech at his last show. Gorgeous George McKay no-showed leaving Dizzy Davis, "a lone wrestling wolf not hooked up with McLemore or Sigel, taking the starring role." According to the story, "Irwin wound up his two-minute intermission speech by announcing that he had been forced to call off the Casino shows because he'll not be able to obtain any more wrestlers."

Irwin went back to boxing, promoting cards in that sport. However, in 1955, he sued Sigel and McLemore. From the *Dallas Morning News* on June 25, 1955: "A $208,000 anti-trust suit was filed in federal court here against wrestling promoters Ed McLemore of Dallas and Morris Sigel and Frank Burke of Houston. Jack Irwin, who, with McLemore, used to promote wrestling shows in Corpus Christi, filed the suit. Irwin's petition said the suit arises out of a conspiracy to monopolize the wrestling business in Texas and to exclude competitors. Irwin had not staged any bouts since May 1954, when McLemore stopped providing him with wrestlers, he says."

The lawsuit laid out the finances of the promotion: "McLemore was to take 55 percent of the gate and pay the wrestlers, while Irwin was to get 45 percent and also be assured by McLemore that he would take no loss, the petition adds. Irwin says McLemore promised him big profits. Between April 28, 1953, and May 26, 1954, Irwin staged 54 shows in Corpus Christi and invested $19,570.48, he says. 'In May 1954, the defendants entered into a conspiracy to monopolize the promotion, booking, exhibition, broadcasting and telecasting of professional wrestling contests and exhibitions through a conspiracy to exclude competition,' the petition declares. Corpus Christi, like other Texas cities where the wrestling war raged, had two wrestling cards and arenas in use during the period in which Irwin staged 54 bouts. Now there is only one. Under the anti-trust laws, Irwin seeks triple damages. His claim is based on the $19,570.46 he says he invested and lost plus $50,000 profits which he says were denied him. That's $69,570.46 And three times that is $208,711.38."

June 25, Joe Scherrer weighed in, with the subhead, "Jack Irwin Says 'See My Lawyer'" and a recap that twice quoted Irwin saying he had nothing to say except the legal referral. Scherrer used the facts from the initial story, credited as being from the Associated Press, and made his own observations. "That $208,721 figure looks somewhat out of line. But Jack wasn't talking and there wasn't any way to check the figures this morning with the Federal Court in Dallas. Jack's shows packed them in for a while. McLemore carried on his war with Sigel for a little over a year. Then McLemore and Sigel buried the hatchet. McLemore folded his circuit. Irwin was one of the last of the McLemore boys to go down. He staged his last show at the Casino one year ago in May. Why was the suit filed in Dallas and not in Corpus Christi? Jack may have the answer. But his only reply this morning was: 'See my lawyer.'"

The newspapers don't mention the lawsuit again, and when Irwin is mentioned in Corpus Christi in the future, it is as a boxing promoter. As for his wrestling career, perhaps in 1955, Irwin finally took a payout from the Texas Wrestling Agency. Either way, he had the most success of any of the McLemore promoters, and yet, he was the last one who seemed to know the truth in May of 1954. The war was over. However, in wrestling, there is always another war.

Inside Information On Wrestling Battle

Dan Cook's

Column

Two Sox Greats

SAN ANTONIO NEWS SPORTS

Credits: San Antonio Evening News, Aug. 10, 1959, column by Dan Cook, art by Bob Dale

10
Pinkie's War

In the late 1950s, Pinkie George had a falling out with the organization he created, the National Wrestling Alliance, and the man who succeeded him as president, Sam Muchnick. George was losing his Iowa towns to rival promoters and felt the NWA was not protecting him. His health was failing, too. So, George decided to leave Iowa and move to San Antonio. Then the man who bitterly complained for years about other promoters encroaching on his territory decided to promote wrestling against the established Livengood-Brown team.

However, Pinky didn't make this decision alone. The San Antonio promoters had been having problems with the Houston office over booking issues and over talent fees. Each side accused the other of being in breach of agreement. So, into San Antonio, as a front for George, came Norman Clark, the Galveston promoter and Morris Sigel brother-in-law, who was also the opposition promoter in Dallas for Sigel. However, because of the contract between the Texas Wrestling Agency and the San Antonio office, Sigel continued to supply talent to Livengood and Brown.

Glenn Pratt summed up the problem in a *San Antonio News* column July 24, 1959: "It seems that Houston wrestling kingpin Morris Sigel, who has been affiliated with (Frank) Brown and Dorathy (Livengood) in San Antonio wrestling for some 20 years, has decided there isn't enough grappling to satisfy the needs of local mat fans."

The article said Clark would run Wednesdays at the Municipal Auditorium beginning Aug. 5. Wednesday had been the traditional night for shows at the Wrestlethon, and promoter Frank Brown said he had a challenge on his hands trying to continue with Sigel against him. "(Sigel) will throw some sort of championship match and some women on his first card, I predict," Brown said in the story. "(Sigel) gets paid for producing wrestling for events in a number of cities. I guess he feels he's got a better deal going for him with Clark. Sure, we're going to have some trouble getting matches of the best quality. And, besides all this, I don't think San Antonio can ... support (two) wrestling matches each week. It's too much. Right now we're doing okay. Some weeks we're the only city in the area to show a profit, even over Fort Worth and Dallas. But two is too many."

Brown said he would like to discuss the matter directly with Sigel, but "(Sigel) wouldn't show up. He's too excitable. He'd probably just send some of his stooges."

Aug. 10, 1959, the legendary San Antonio columnist Dan Cook wrote about "Inside Information About Wrestling Battle" in his column in the *San Antonio News*: "Battle lines are drawn. Troops are all in formation. The first shots were fired last week. No casualties have yet been reported. The wrestling war is underway. It all started two weeks ago with the announcement that new promoters would venture into the field offering opposition to Dorathy Livengood and Frank Brown, who in reality are Mr. and Mrs. Before it's over more than the wrestlers will be groaning. This promises to be a strange and interesting 'war' because Morris Sigel, longtime kingpin of Texas wrestling circles, is feeding ammunition to both sides. Sigel, who heads the booking agency in Houston that channels all 'union' matmen, is supplying both promoters here. Therefore it becomes obvious which side Sigel himself had taken. If he did not want a new promoter to buck his old associate, Frank Brown, Sigel needed only to refuse him talent. If more evidence as to Sigel's choice is wanted it can be obtained simply by looking to the new promoter. His name is Norman Clark and he happens to be Sigel's brother-in-law. So the war, you might say, really is between Sigel and Frank Brown. You might also say that if this is the case it should be a short war. Sigel could cut off Brown's supply line — quit sending him wrestlers — and Brown would be forced from business. But there's a little matter about anti-trust laws and both sides are familiar with these legal rules. Sigel can't cut Brown off and fatten up Brown's competitor without facing serious lawsuits. So, Morris must continue to ship talent in to both sides — to the Auditorium on Wednesdays and to the Wrestlethon on Thursdays.

"Clark is little more than a figurehead here. He has the license in his name only because Pinky George, listed as matchmaker, hasn't been in Texas long enough to own promoting papers. George is putting up the money for the Auditorium and in the long run it will be Pinky George who will sink or swim. George, a mild, distinguished-looking little gent, has a long list of successful promotions in his wake. A former resident of Des Moines, Iowa, he came here for his health. To better a bad sinus condition. It was hardly more than fate that sent him stumbling into Sigel's offer to buck Brown and go into the wrestling dodge. George is still listed as a director on the old Waterloo Hawks basketball team in the NBA. He still has the franchise on the Des Moines ice hockey team in the United States league but his son Paul operates it. George was

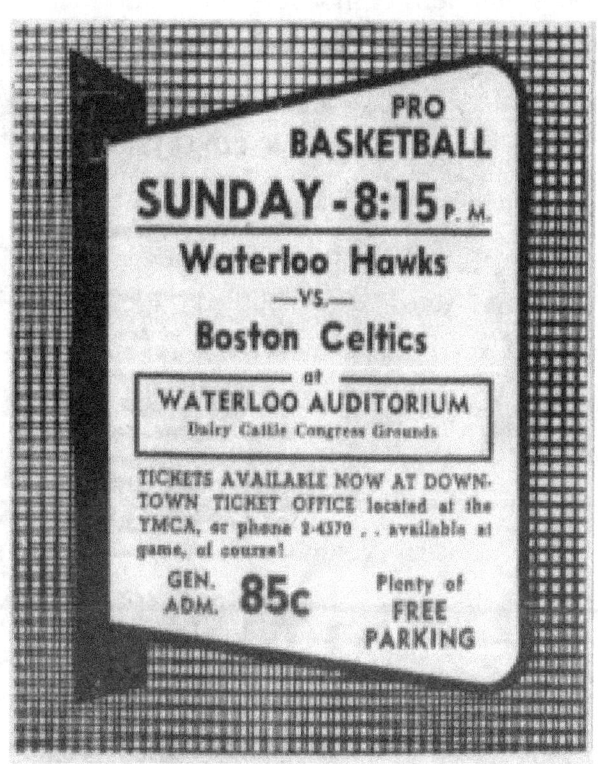

Pinkie George's NBA team in Waterloo, Iowa, lasted a single season, 1949-50.

— and still is — a manager of boxers. He once tutored such men as Johnny Paycheck, Lee Savold and Glenn Flannagan. I tell you these things only because George is the newcomer. He needs an introduction in this area. Brown, on the other hand, has been operating very successfully at the Wrestlethon for 20 years and folks hereabouts are familiar with him or his deeds."

The column includes the Bob Dale cartoon that is on the cover of this book, where Sigel is tossing wrestlers to both George and Brown. Cook concludes that two promotions cannot survive in San Antonio in the long term and sums up the strengths and weaknesses of each: "George has in his favor the firm hand of Sigel and the fact that bus-riders need no transfers to get to his Auditorium. Brown has in his favor a well-established trade and his own arena. While George must put out $200 rent and get nothing back on concession sales, Brown has no rent problem and keeps all concession cash."

Pinkie George in 1959.

Cook ended the column with a quote from each of the principals. Sigel: "Brown has been trying to organize the wrestlers for some time. They're already organized and no additional help from him is needed. For some time now he's felt he hasn't needed me. Good. I certainly don't need him."

Brown: "I think the whole thing is a misunderstanding. I've tried to talk to Sigel twice in recent months but never can seem to reach him. We're going about our business over here just like we have for 20 years and we hope to continue doing so."

George: "I'm not sore at anyone. I'm just a businessman in business here. No one gets excited if they open a fourth, fifth or sixth bank in San Antonio. Why should it be so newsworthy because we have two wrestling promoters here? I like it and I'm here to stay."

In the ring, the vision Cook and Brown shared came true, leading to the newcomers getting an advantage. Wrestlingdata.com has attendance figures for a half dozen cards from each promoter in the late summer of 1959. George's debut show Wednesday, Aug. 5, at the Auditorium drew 1,258 fans for a main event of El Enfermero over George Bollas. The next day at the Wrestlethon, 884 fans saw Jack O'Brien beat Dick Raines. Somehow, O'Brien worked both shows the next week. Aug. 12 at the Aud, he lost to El Enfermero, while Danny McShain beat Alex Perez before 917 fans. The next night at the Wrestlethon, 894 fans saw Stu Gibson beat Raines and O'Brien beat Ivan the Terrible. The next week saw an odd shift: only 973 fans saw Lou Thesz beat McShain on Wednesday while 1,440 fans saw Ivan beat Gibson on Thursday. There is no card listed for the Auditorium on Aug. 27. Gibson got revenge on Ivan at the Wrestlethon on the 28th but no attendance is listed.

In September, the crowds flipped again. Wednesday the 2nd, 1,620 fans saw Pepper Gomez beat George Bollas and the Kozak brothers, Nick and Jerry, beat the Corsicans. Thursday the 3rd, 782 fans saw O'Brien beat Gibson. The next Tuesday, Ivan appeared at the Aud, teaming with Zebra Kid on the losing side against Gomez and Nick Kozak before another 1,620 fans. Cook listed the Thursday attendance at about 500 at the Wrestlethon, where Dizzy Davis topped Luis Hernandez in the main event.

Cook chimed in again, in a column on Sept. 14. "The cold war on the wrestling front can be expected to get very hot in the near future. General George, the matchmaker they call Pinkie, has rolled up his heavy artillery in the form of name attractions such as James Braddock, Jack Dempsey and world mat champ Pat O'Connor. The move has been expensive — and not yet profitable — but enemy losses have been heavy. On the other side of the battlefield, General Brown, the matchmaker named Frank, has held the line despite a mounting casualty list. It is now believed that he is planning a new strategy and about ready to launch a counter-attack. He and his underground agents have carefully mapped out a new supply line and reports indicate he will soon break completely with Morris Sigel in Houston. President Sigel, the booking agent for wrestling hands in this southwest area, has been supplying both sides with talent. But this has grown confusing to the wrestlers as well as the fans."

Cook lamented that the boys sometimes don't know if they are good guys or bad guys, or which feuds they are in, noting how some wrestlers have worked on both sides of the battle. And if the boys are confused, he mused, what must the fans be thinking?

"There's no love lost between Brown and Sigel despite the fact they've been doing business together for 20 years. In Houston, Sigel accused Brown of trying to set up his own booking agency and taking over as top man. That caused the break. Brown denied the accusation but it makes little difference now which man was right. More than likely Brown is now ready to attempt what he was accused of earlier. Less than 500 attended Brown's Wrestlethon show last Thursday — his smallest crowd in a long time. He is expected to now turn to Arizona or some other agency in the area for his future talent. If this is correct — and I believe it is — Brown will have to grab new territory down here from under the thumb of Sigel. Wrestlers cannot come all the way from Arizona just for one night's work in San Antonio. Pound for pound the average wrestler is worth far less than T-bone steak for a night's work. The preliminary matman receives about $50 a night, according to the crowd. So, he must be guaranteed at least two other working dates in the area or he will stay home. At the present there aren't two other spots in the area that area not ruled by Sigel. So Brown may have to establish new beachheads. The results should prove interesting. Probably more so than at any other time since Jack Hammonds, the 'Holler for Hammonds' insurance man, started pro wrestling bouts here in a tent on the old Exposition grounds."

Whatever turnaround Brown had hoped for, it did not happen immediately.

Sept. 16, the Aud attendance hit a new high for fans, 2,100 according to Sigel. They came to see Gomez get a shot at NWA champion Pat O'Connor. Tied at a fall each, they were both counted out in the third fall. Duke Keomuka and Mr. Moto beat the Kozak brothers in the semifinal. The next night was another low point for the Wrestlethon at 528 fans for a main event of Totina and Joe Hanley over Bob Gourley and Bob Stovall.

Pat O'Connor in 1956. Greg Oliver Collection

The amazing thing about the Jack Pfefer collection at the Father Ted Hesburgh Library's Rare Books and Special Collections Department is all of the main players in the San Antonio war wrote to Pfefer, and did so at least once each during the San Antonio war. So, as Cook did in his columns, Pfefer got all sides of the narration on what turned out to be a six-month battle.

From Brown on Sept. 1, 1959: "Dear Jack, A few months ago you wrote to me and asked what was going on in Texas, that they would not book your men, etc., what was going on behind the scenes, etc. As you know, I never answered your letter and I think now you know why I didn't. If by chance you don't know, let me explain. For quite a long time now, Sigel has been increasingly disturbed because I demanded what I felt was rightfully mine, for the 10% I paid. When they wouldn't let me have a match that I knew would draw for me, I raised (devil). In each case, it burned them up until Sigel got the idea of getting rid of

24 San Antonio Light
Friday, Aug. 7, 1959

Wrestling

Round One Goes to New Promoters

Round one in the battle between rival wrestling promoters went to the newcomers—Norman Clark and Pinkie George.

Their show at the municipal auditorium Wednesday night attracted 1250 cash customers while only 884 showed up for the Dorothy Livengood-Frank Brown Thursday night session at the Wrestlethon. The auditorium take at the box office was $1563 gross while the Wrestlethon did $1369.75 worth of business.

Before Clark and George moved in, the Wrestlethon had been averaging about 1400 fans per week, although some shows had dipped as low as 1000.

As their next attraction, Livengood and Brown will present a 4-man tag team bout pitting Stu Gibson and Dick Raines against Jack O'Brien and Ivan the Terrible. As an added attraction, after the event, Jack O'Brien will face Byron Cacbols.

O'Brien decisioned Dick Raines in Thursday main event. Gibson beat Ivan the Terrible, but since the timekeeper interfered, the wrestling commissioner ruled it "no decision." In other bouts, Pedro Godoy defeated Tonina, Luis Hernandez drew with Bennie Matla and Angelo Martinelli pinned Ed Sharpe.

COOK'S TOUR WITH DAN COOK

The Mat Battle

THE COLD WAR ON THE wrestling front can be expected to get very hot in the near future.

General George, the matchmaker they call Pinkie, has rolled up his heavy artillery in the form of name attractions such as James Braddock, Jack Dempsey and world mat champ Pat O'Connor. The move has been expensive—and not yet profitable—but enemy losses have been heavy.

FRANK BROWN

On the other side of the battlefield, General Brown, the matchmaker named Frank, has held the line despite a mounting casualty list. It is now believed that he is planning new strategy and about ready to launch a counter-attack. He and his underground agents have carefully mapped out a new supply line and reports indicate he will soon break completely with Morris Sigel in Houston.

President Sigel, the booking agent for wrestling hands in this southwest area, has been supplying both sides with talent. But this has grown confusing to the wrestlers as well as to fans.

Like all good shows or comic strips, wrestling bouts on a weekly basis must have some continuity. But with many of the same faces appearing on different cards in the same town it's difficult to determine a "goodie" from a "baddie." That is to say, promoters must build "grudge" matches from week-to-week and keep the fires well fanned if they are to create customer interest and gate appeal.

Such is hard to do with different promoters and different ideas in the same town using the same wrestlers.

And too, in the heat of a battle some matmen are apt to forget from day to day whether or not it's their turn to be a good guy or a bad guy.

THERE'S NO LOVE LOST between Brown and Sigel despite the fact they've been doing business together for [illegible] years. In Houston Sigel accused Brown of trying to set up his own booking agency and taking over as top man. That caused the break.

Brown denied the accusation but it makes little difference now which man was right. More than likely Brown is now ready to attempt what he was accused of earlier.

Less than [illegible] attended Brown's Wrestlathon show last Thursday—his smallest crowd in a long time. He is expected to now turn to Arizona or some other agency in that area for his future talent.

If this is correct—and I believe it is—Brown will have to grab new territory down here from under the thumb of Sigel. Wrestlers cannot come all the way from Arizona just for one night's work in San Antonio.

POUND-FOR-POUND THE average wrestler is worth far less than T-bone steak for a night's work. The preliminary matmen receives about [illegible] a night, according to the crowd. So he must be guaranteed at least two other working dates in the area or he'll stay home.

At the present there aren't two other spots in the area that are not ruled by Sigel. So Brown may have to establish new beachheads.

The results should prove interesting. Probably more so than

Credits:

1) San Antonio Light, Aug. 7, 1959
2) San Antonio Evening News, Sept. 14, 1959

me. This he started weeks ago by coming into San Antonio and promoting against me. I knew he was going to pull something on me sometime, but I didn't know just when, and because of this, I was caught unprepared. I have been booking with Houston since they came in here but as you know this can be an impossible set-up, as they tell boys not to lose, etc., making it impossible to work programs. Jack, you will remember when you were in Sigel's office he had you call me and talk to me and imply he, Sigel, was going to maybe come in with you, against me. Remember he talked of my having a booking office, etc.? It was all in his plan evidentially (sic) at that time, to try and take over my town. What I am showing you Jack why I didn't answer your letter. Sigel was using every excuse he could to try and show I was trying to take over, so that when he double-crossed me, it would look as though I was the one causing the trouble, but I think this has backfired, as now after five weeks, all know who double crossed whom. I say it has backfired on him as the letters and calls we have received from around the country strongly side with us. They have tried to spread lies about us but those who know the facts can easily see the lies so they are wasting time there, but always as is such in a case like this, many, many things unpleasant happen, I will not go into more here."

Brown concludes by telling Pfefer the Houston office is afraid of him and does not want to give him too much power in Texas by booking his wrestlers.

Pfefer didn't just tell Sigel about Brown's words; he mailed him the entire letters from Brown. Sept. 8, 1959, from Sigel to Pfefer: "Received your letter and I want to thank you for your co-operation. In this business co-operation is rare and it is good to know who your friends are when the chips are down. The letter you sent was full of the same kind of double talk that this fellow has been handing to boys all over the country. You know the truth of the matter, that he was all set to double cross the people who had made him a fortune over the years and was caught, as he says, unprepared. You will recall that we phoned you when we first heard about this and you gave some excellent advice. We took it and instead of waiting to be hit on the head with a hammer we went into action.

The results are gratifying. We now have our own TV show, a studio show. He is about to lose his television time. Last week we drew $1,900 in the Auditorium on Wednesday, he drew $1,200 in his building on Thursday. These are the facts and the correct figures no matter what you may hear from him."

Sigel ended the letter reversing the accusation about who did not want Pfefer in Texas, blaming Brown. He wrote a P.S.: "We are still furnishing him his talent and that is the only reason why he is alive at all."

Brown wrote Pfefer again Sept 12, 1959: "Concerning Sigel's double cross of me here. He is furnishing men to Pinky George who is supposed to be the matchmaker. They had Norman Clark of Galveston get a promoter's license as Pinky George was not a resident of Texas and could not get a promoter's license. Actually, Paul Boesch, Sidney Balkin and the whole Houston office is trying to promote the town. They are running in the Municipal Auditorium where we used to run before we built our arena. How long they will run there is questionable as it is a political set-up and anything could happen. Because of Sigel's actions, he is forcing me to go on my own which I know will be tough but then one can not just let a person run them out of business. Attached is a photostatic copy of a letter to Stu Gibson, who works for me. I am sending the copy because Sigel has been spreading the bull that we wrote a lot of boys asking them to come in and work for us in a booking office. The only letters ever written asking boys to come in were the ones Burke asked us to write. Thought this might help straighten out one of the lies they have been telling."

Pfefer again sent Sigel the letter from Brown, which Sigel noted he was returning for Pfefer's files. From a Sigel letter marked Sept. 15, 1959: "There's not much to tell you about the situation in San Antonio. Pinkie continues to out-draw the others 2 to 1. I am enclosing a clipping from San Antonio which I am sure you will enjoy reading, I believe he had ideas of getting talent out of Tucson, but from what I understand, there is no talent to speak of obtainable ... and ... those fellows have some troubles of their own ... and are not interested, nor do they have time to devote to someone else's fight." After some other busi-

Tag Match Set Saturday

Something new awaits San Antonio wrestling fans Saturday night at the Wrestlethon Arena — an eight-man tag team match.

Two men from each team will be in the ring at the same time, Matchmaker Frank Brown said.

Stu Gibson, Tonina, Benny Matta and Indio Poon are members of one team. The other includes Dizzy Davis, Lucifer, Sammy Baldwin and the Blue Demon.

The main eventers will pair off for one-fall preliminary bouts, the opponents to be picked by a drawing.

The show-opener will be for one fall or 20 minutes and will match Doug Kinslow against Manuel Guerra.

BOXING

ASSOCIATED PRESS

WRESTLING
WED. 8:30 P.M.
AUDITORIUM
WORLD'S TAG TEAM CHAMPIONSHIP
KEOMUKA and MR. MOTO
— VS —
GOMEZ, ANAYA
4 OTHER STAR BOUTS
$1.00—$1.50—$2.00
For Tickets . . . CA 7-7491
MUNICIPAL AUDITORIUM

Credits:
1) San Antonio Evening News, Nov. 17, 1959, article for Livengood-Brown show, across from ad for Burke-George show

1959 San Antonio NEWS

Mat Tourney Slated Here

Twelve wrestlers will compete in a one-night tournament on Saturday night's program at the Wrestlethon Arena, Matchmaker Frank Brown announced Monday.

They are Dizzy Davis, Stu Gibson, Benny Matta, Sheik Omar, Tonina, Joe Castillo, Gus Eddis, Lou Plummer, Lucifer, Manuel Guerra, Luis (Blue Demon) Trinidad and Indio Poon.

The tourney will include 11 matches, all for one fall or 15 minutes except the finale, which will be wrestled to a finish.

Each wrestler will put up an entry fee of $50 and the Wrestlethon management will add $400 to the pot, assuring the winner of a $1,000 purse, Brown said.

Quail Shooting

Gibson Will Meet Tonina

The main event on Saturday night's mat program at the Wrestlethon will match Stu Gibson against Tonina, Matchmaker Frank Brown announced Monday.

Gibson will substitute for Dizzy Davis, who was injured here last week.

The top bout will be for two out of three falls and have a time limit of one hour.

Other matches will be for one fall and will be Benny Matta vs. Sheik Omar, Indio Poon vs. Ollie Kauri, Gene Eddis vs. Joe Castillo, and Lee Coy vs. Manuel Guerra.

The first match will be at 8:30 p.m.

Credits: 2) Ad for Burke-George show, Jan. 12, 1960
3) San Antonio Evening News, Dec. 29, 1959
4) San Antonio Evening News, Jan. 12, 1960

ness, Sigel concluded: "I want to thank you so much for your helpfulness and assure you that it is always a pleasure to hear from you."

Sigel wrote again and returned another Brown letter Sept. 21, 1959: "Pinkie actually drew $2,100 ... he is going up each week ... while Brown is coming down. It's a funny thing how double-crossers always start crying when the going gets tough ... but I guess that is part of the game. Pinkie called just after I read your letter, and I gave him your greetings ... and asked that he mail his program to you."

The next letter in the file is from Sigel on Oct. 28, 1959: "Dear Jack, I haven't written you because there is actually nothing to report from the Front Line! Looks like we just have a little 'Brush War' in San Antonio. ... Pinkie is out-drawing them 2 to 1 ... the only thing that keeps them going is the fact that they own their building and have little expenses. They have run a few shows outside of San Antonio but drew nothing ... a little over $100 in one of them recently. It seems to me that it is just a question of time before they eliminate themselves."

In October, Brown moved his shows to Saturday night. He ran twice one week, Thursday, Oct. 8, and Saturday, Oct. 10, as part of the transition. It may have helped to have his show on a weekend, or at least not back to back against the show with the established talent.

Wednesday, Oct. 21, 1,805 fans saw the O'Connor-Gomez rematch. The next week, Gomez and Blackie Guzman challenged Moto and Keomuka for the Texas Tag Team Titles. Yet, all was not well. George could only get the Auditorium for six dates through the end of the year.

The calendar to begin 1960 was even worse. However, his biggest problem had to do with finances. His shows were reportedly losing money. By December, with the war cooling, Brown's letter to Pfefer mentions nothing about Sigel or George. Instead, he recommends a worker from the Arizona crew, Indio Peon, as a potential ethnic star for Pfefer.

As the new year approached, Sigel and Brown apparently finally spoke. A deal was worked out to give George a soft landing into promoting boxing. The

COOK'S TOUR WITH DAN COOK

Promoter's Wrestling War Ends Here

EXCLUSIVE

Friend Jack: A deal was made + I'm out! — Regards Pinkie

COOK'S TOUR WITH DA

Promoter's Wrestling W

EXCLUSIVE

Credits:

1) Dan Cook column, San Antonio Evening News, Feb. 2, 1960

2) Clipping of Dan Cook column with note from Pinkie George to Jack Pfefer, courtesy of the Rare Books and SpecialCollections Department, Hesburgh Libraries, University of Notre Dame

San Antonio Light columnist Harold Scherwicz went in-depth on the resolution in his column on Feb. 4, 1960. The section begins "Speaking of money, Wrestling Promoter Frank Brown whose Wrestlethon arena shows will go back to Wednesday night next week (not a month hence) now that Pinkie George has closed up shop at the Municipal Auditorium following the 'cease fire' between Brown and Southwestern Mat Czar Morris Sigel of Houston: 'This misunderstanding between me and Mr. Sigel should never have happened. I knew it all along but it was my cue to sit back and wait for things to cool off. They have, and everything is all right again. We are going back to Wednesday night, our wrestling night for 23 years. Mr. Sigel held the strong hand, as anybody worth $7,000,000 would do.' Then Promoter Brown said: 'We made money while two shows a week were going on. But I figure I lost $20,000 in the six months Mr. George was in operation. That's $20,000 I would have made more than I did.' Simple arithmetic shows then that the Brown operation ordinarily makes $40,000 a year plus the profits, unstated that came in while the 'war' was on. Hmmmm! What about George? Poor Pinkie! He's pleased as punch that Sigel has discontinued the mat shows he ran in opposition to Brown. Now he has time to devote to his heavyweight fighter, Alejandro Lavorante, to his several apartment buildings in Des Moines, to the hockey team he owns, to the booking agency that handles the Globetrotters and other shows in Iowa, to Des Moines wrestling etc. A sad case."

Dan Cook weighed in Feb. 2, with a column headlined "Promoter's Wrestling War Ends Here." The piece was short on details but certain about the aftermath: "It's difficult to determine just which side surrendered but secret meetings this week are certain to result in two obvious moves — Frank Brown will continue to operate at the Wrestlethon and Pinky George will discontinue his Municipal Auditorium operations." Cook notes that the dispute between Sigel and Brown began the war, and that no one had officially confirmed the end of the war to him. "The Wrestlethon matchmaker will be reluctant to claim a victory while it is expected George will never admit defeat in this business scrap that lasted several months. It can be assumed that both men suffered financial losses. Brown's Wrestlethon crowds dwindled in half at times and George had trouble reserving each Wednesday night date at the expensive Auditorium. During the next five weeks only one Wednesday night is available for wrestling with other events booking the house months in advance."

Amazingly, there is a clipping of this column in the Pfefer collection with a short note from George written on the top. "Friend Jack: A deal was made + I'm Out! - Regards, Pinkie" read the note.

Sigel wrote again to Pfefer on Feb. 18, 1960, mostly to congratulate Pfefer on a good crowd, but he added a coda to the San Antonio war: "Yes, everything is all straightened out in San Antonio. Frank Brown took care of Pinkie in a nice way ... Pinkie is going to promote some fights in San Antonio ... and as far as I know, everyone is happy over the situation."

For quite a long time now,Sigel has been increasingly disturbed because I demanded what I felt was rightfully mine,for the 10% I paid.When they wouldn't let me have a match that I knew would draw for me,I raised the deveil.In each case it burned them up until Sigel got the idea of getting rid of me.This he started 5 weeks ago by coming into San Antonio and promoting against me.I knew he was going to pull something on me sometime,but I didn't know just when,and because of this,I was caught unprepared.I have been booking with Houston since they came in here but as you know this can be an impossible set-up,as they tell boys not to lose,etc.,making it impossible to work programs.

Jack,you will remember when you were in Sigel's office, he had you call me and talk to me and imply he,Sigel, was going to maybe come in with you,against me. Remember he talked of my having a booking office,etc.? It was all in his plan,evidentally at that time,to try and take over my town.What I am showing you Jack is why I didn't answer you letter.Sigel was using every excuse he could to try and show I was tryingto take over,so that when he double-crossed me,it would look as though I was the one causing the trouble,but I think this has badfired,as now after 5 weeks,all know who double-crossed whom.I say it has backfired on him as the letters and calls we have received from around the country strongly side with us.

Credits:
1) Sept. 1, 1959, Frank Brown letter to Jack Pfefer.
which Pfefer sent to Morris Sigel.
Sigel read it and sent it back to Pfefer.
Courtesy of the
Rare Books and Special Collections Department,
Hesburgh Libraries, University of Notre Dame

LIVENGOOD-BROWN ENTERPRISES

The Wrestlethon

Phone CA 6-1529 405 E. Josephine

SAN ANTONIO, TEXAS

Concerning Sigel's double-cross of me here.He is furnishing men to Pinky George who is supposed to be the matchmaker.They had Norman Clark of Galveston get a promoter's license as Pinky George was not a resident of Texas and could not get a promoter's license.Actually Paul Boesch,Sidney Balkin and the whole Houston Office is trying to promte the town. They are running in the Municipal Auditorium where we used to run before we built our arena.How long they will run there is questionable asit is a political set-up and anything could happen.Because of Sigel's actions,he is forcing me to go on my own which I know will be tough but then one can not just let a person run them out of business.

Best regards,

Frank

Frank Brown

Credits:
1) Sept. 12, 1959, Frank Brown letter to Jack Pfefer. which Pfefer sent to Morris Sigel. Sigel read it and sent it back to Pfefer.
Courtesy of the Rare Books and Special Collections Department, Hesburgh Libraries, University of Notre Dame

PAUL BOESCH TAKES OVER WRESTLING
With Shirley Carriger, Daughter of Morris Sigel
—Post Photo

Boesch To Take Over Mat Promotion Here

Paul Boesch, who was associated with the late Morris Sigel in promoting wrestling matches here for many years, announced at a Friday press conference at the Rice Hotel that he had purchased the Gulf Athletic Club, which stages the bouts in Houston.

The sale must be approved by the City Council, due to leasing arrangements which the Club has with the city.

Boesch, who also is well-known here as a writer and civic worker, said Mrs Irene Sigel, wife of the deceased Morris Sigel, had asked him to carry on with the wrestling promotion.

"Wrestling has always taken pride in giving fans more than their money's worth," said Boesch. "I intend to expand that practice. It will be a new era of wrestling."

The Gulf Athletic Club has moved to new offices at 2022 San Jacinto at Gray. The phone number remains CA 2-2388.

11
The Aftermath

In his recounting of the history of Houston Wrestling, Paul Boesch's nephew Peter Birkholz noted the 1960s were a time of turbulence in wrestling as in society. In Houston, the City Auditorium was torn down in 1963 and the matches moved full time to the Sam Houston Coliseum. However, it took time for the promotion to establish the Coliseum as the new home. Plus, it took a lot more fans to fill up the 10,000-plus seat Coliseum than it did the 4,000-plus seat Aud.

In 1964, the promotion grew worried enough it brought Jack Pfefer in to try to turn things around. Pfefer took offense to something and ended up leaving Texas quickly. The implication in a letter he wrote to Morris Sigel is Pfefer had a falling out with Boesch.

Boesch, for his part, always praised Pfefer for giving him a start in the business, while also noting his shady business practices, something he often contrasted with Sigel's sterling reputation in Houston.

"He affected my life like no other man," Boesch said in his book. "He gave me my start in wrestling."

However: "Pfefer stood about five feet tall and weighed about a hundred pounds, a striking contrast to the giants he tried to keep under his managerial thumb. Because of the things he did back in the '30s, Pfefer is responsible for much of the attitude of doubt that fans have had toward wrestling. It is to the ever-lasting credit of most promoters and wrestlers that they resisted following the path he carelessly carved and regained the respect of the fans. He had few scruples and justified his excesses by firmly believing he was doing the fans a favor when he gave a match added flavor."

One of the letters in the Hesburgh collection is from Doc Sarpolis to Pfefer sympathizing with his hurt feelings from his treatment in Houston. "Concerning your letter, you know how I feel about this stabbing in the back guy. ... You know how I feel about your intense aggravation that you experienced in Houston. I felt that way at one time, too. But I got rid of the whole mess by splitting up my partnership with Morris and Frank. I hope that Morris someday will find that the knife is ready for him, too, and prevent it from being plunged into his back also."

By then, Sarpolis had his own territory, having bought Amarillo in 1955 from Dory Detton. Sarpolis gave the newspapers a different reason for his leaving the TWA partnership with Sigel and Burke than he did to Pfefer. And there is some irony in a man who at least three times tried to help take the booking agency away from Sigel, lamenting how Sigel hopefully won't feel the knife from Boesch. Still, Sarpolis leaving Dallas in 1954 for the motel business may owe more to "the stabbing in the back guy" than trouble patching things up with Sigel and Burke.

At the end of 1964, desperate to make something happen, the Houston promotion gambled on a controversial angle. Fritz Von Erich, the master of the Iron Claw, applied his killer hold to the referee. When Boesch, the television announcer, questioned Von Erich about his actions, Von Erich clawed Boesch, too. Attendance spiked through 1965 as Houston Wrestling played one of its favorite booking games: Who can stop this monster heel? Bull Curry, Ernie Ladd, Johnny Valentine and others had main event matches with Von Erich. Attendances popped. The Sam Houston Coliseum was established as one of wrestling's key venues.

By the mid-1960s, Von Erich was the biggest star in Texas. He was also a protege of Ed McLemore, the guy recommended to Jack Pfefer by Tommy "Your Boy Izzy" Phelps. His base was Dallas. In September 1966, Morris Sigel had

An autographed photo of "The German Bomber" Fritz Von Erich. Courtesy Heritage Auctions, HA.com

another heart attack, this once essentially fatal, as he died in December. At this point, Sigel's longtime rivals made their move. From Muchnick's winter newsletter to NWA promoters: "It is my understanding that the Houston and Dallas offices have worked out an amiable agreement. Morris Sigel will continue as the promoter in Houston, Texas, while the office of Ed McLemore will do the booking for Dallas, Fort Worth, Houston, Austin, Beaumont and cities in that area. As soon as I get more facts will keep you fully informed. Ed McLemore's address is Cadiz and Industrial, Dallas, Texas."

In San Antonio, the Livengood-Brown team had begun to build its own circuit within the Texas loop, and they also broke off from Sigel months before his death.

Dan Cook shared details when he paid respects to Sigel in his Dec. 29, 1966, column: "The king is dead. Morris Pincus Sigel, one-time failure as a clerk and long-time ruler of wrestling in Texas, died Tuesday and will be buried in Houston today. Not many San Antonians knew Mr. Sigel but for many years his heavy hand directed wrestling traffic here. And in just about every other Texas spot where professional matmen toil. Morris, you see, had a hammerlock on the game and he kept a tight grip on it until the last years when a series of heart attacks left him a tired old man. He was 69 and in his 50th year of promoting in Houston when the last attack came. Long ago Sigel became sort of a booking agent for all pro wrestlers who visited Texas. You used his guys or you lost his favor. Sometimes it got very expensive to lose favor with Mr. Sigel."

The column described Sigel as non-athletic but extremely competitive. It went on to detail the recent changes in wrestling locally. "Four months ago San Antonio promoter Frank Brown decided to use talent other than that provided by Morris. It wasn't an original plan but from such deeds wrestling wars often spring. Before the first non-Sigel import could be introduced here Morris had me on the phone."

Cook then ran down the exchange:

"Dan, you know somebody over there who'd like to promote wrestling? I'll furnish all the wrestlers and make it right so nobody will lose any money."

"No, Morris, offhand I can't think of anybody. What's the matter with Frank Brown? Isn't he promoting here anymore?"

"He is. But he's doing so without my boys. I intend to give him a little opposition until he learns a lesson."

"You mean we get another wrestling war?"

"Call it what you want but the time has come for Mr. Brown to learn another lesson."

Instead, Sigel died, leaving Cook to eulogize: "Morris, like all of us, had his faults. Sometimes he played the game a little too rough. Even for the rough business world. But he was a friend of mine to the end. Not a close friend. But certainly a good friend."

Less than two weeks after Sigel died, his biggest attraction, the depression-era hillbilly Whiskers Savage, also passed away. If it was a signal that an era had ended, it was not the only one. Ed McLemore did not get to enjoy his victory for long. He got sick in early 1968 and died early in 1969. His protege, Fritz Von Erich, ended up benefiting the most from the change in booking office. Fritz controlled Texas for nearly a decade, using that perch to gain power in the National Wrestling Alliance as well. He became president in 1975. Soon after, his sons entered the business, setting the stage for the story we know as the Von Erich tragedy.

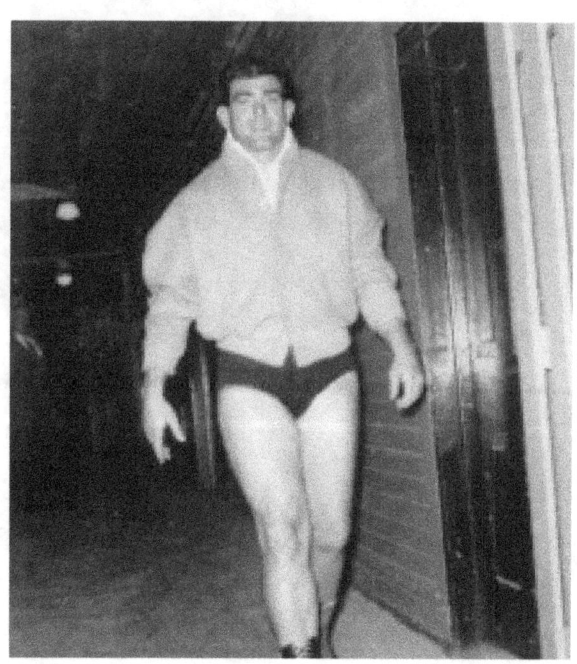

Joe Blanchard in 1957. Greg Oliver Collection

In San Antonio, Livengood and Brown used their victories to create a South Texas loop. By the end of their tenure, they not only promoted San Antonio, but also Austin, Seguin and some towns on the river and gulf. In the late 1960s, they took Joe Blanchard, a Canadian Football League player turned Texas babyface, as their partner. The Wrestle-thon closed in 1967, after the land was taken by the city in order to build a highway. The promotion switched to the Auditorium before finding a home at the Hemisfair Arena. In the meantime, Livengood bought an old Handy Andy store at 1704

Blanco Road to film television matches. The wrestling world knew it as The Junction.

Brown died in 1977 and Livengood sold their shares to Blanchard. She stayed with the promotion, though, helping until it folded, mostly in the ticket office, of course. In the mid-1970s, San Antonio was part of the Texas loop booked by the Dallas office. However, Blanchard quickly broke away and pushed his own group of wrestlers around the South Texas loop. His promotion was aided by cable television and a spot on the USA Network. However, he lost the spot on the cable channel, and it went to the WWF, the expanding World Wrestling Federation led by Vince K. McMahon, who was known to the old guard as Vinnie or Junior. Again, San Antonio and television wrestling were in the middle of a major change in the business.

In Houston, Paul Boesch took over the city promotion but not the state booking office. It has often been said the Sigel and Burke families did not want to continue promoting and willingly sold to Sigel's protege. However, Sigel's daughter Shirley "Lee" Carringer did seem to have an interest in promoting. She was the assistant promoter in Houston at the end of her father's life, and her letters to Jack Pfefer are filled with discussions about wrestlers, matches and crowds.

According to a SLAM! Wrestling article by Greg Oliver about the Christy Brothers tag team, Lee dated Bobby Christy about the time her father died, and she pitched him on them running the territory together. "She said that she knows when her dad passes away that Paul Boesch would get her right out of there, edge her out. If it would have been up to me, had that been my desire, I could have been with her and we probably could have had the Houston territory," he told Oliver.

In reality, Boesch got the promotion and did get Lee out of there. Contrary to the truism that no one disliked Paul Boesch, there is a list of people in this era who either didn't like his booking or felt he played hardball to get the promotion. Of course, Boesch always said he learned his business habits from Sigel. To

THE HOUSTON CHRONICLE

Julius Sigel

25th MORRIS SIGEL'S SILVER ANNIVERSARY

Morris Sigel

Celebrating 25 Years of Service to Houston Sports Fans

MORRIS SIGEL'S 25TH ANNIVERSARY GIFT TO THE WRESTLING FANS

FRIDAY, NOV. 10

AT HOUSTON AUDITORIUM

AN ALL-STAR CARD

AND

EVERY SEAT IN THE HOUSE 25¢

LOOK AT THIS PROGRAM!

Main Event

"IRON MIKE" MAZURKI

Versus

ABE "KING-KONG" KASHEY

Semi-Final

JIM "GOON" HENRY

Versus

HENRY PIERS

FRIENDS AND WELL-WISHERS OF MORRIS SIGEL WHOSE RESPECT MAKES POSSIBLE THIS TRIBUTE

★ Wrestling Program ★

GULF ATHLETIC CLUB, Promoter — MRS. SHIRLEY CARRIGER, Assistant Promoter

No. 1092 — FRIDAY, JANUARY 6, 1967 — HOUSTON, TEXAS — PHONES: CA 2-2388-89 — PRICE: 20 CENTS

A TRIBUTE TO A GREAT PROMOTER…A FINE FRIEND… MORRIS SIGEL LEFT A LIVING LEGACY FOR SPORTS FANS

MORRIS P. SIGEL
31 OCTOBER 1897 –
– 27 DECEMBER 1966

In the early morning hours of Tuesday, December 27, 1966, Morris Sigel died. Thus ended a gallant battle that had been going on since 1952 when he was stricken with his first heart attack.

Morris was not an athlete but hundreds of men of muscle, with sturdy physiques and battered faces, admit that his daily duel with death was waged with a courage they could not have displayed.

In spite of this handicap Morris Sigel maintained his promotional control of wrestling in Houston. The sport was not only his livelihood, it was his hobby and his very life. He came to the office every day, made decisions, contacts and friendships, he looked forward to each day behind his crowded desk.

Unlike most people in the sports world Morris was a quiet and unobtrusive man who went about his business in an easy, orderly manner. But he was also a man who could explode into colorful language and express himself in a way that made the air turn blue when the situation demanded it.

In spite of his small size he was ready to stand up to the biggest of men and voice his opinion when there was a controversy. He was for you or he was against you, there was no middle ground.

And he was just as quick to express friendship. Morris was fiercely loyal to those who were associated with him and prized loyalty in return as a fitting reward.

Morris had a deep sense of feeling for his fellow man and his generosity toward individuals and needy causes was constant. He made philantropy a part of his life although he would never have used such a big word to describe it. He was a "soft touch" in every wonderful sense of the word.

Most things about Morris Sigel are a matter of indisputable record: 50 years of sports promotion; the first wrestling license and the first boxing license in the State of Texas; commendations from the State legislature and from hundreds of organizations for his great help to people who needed it; innovations in the wrestling game that have become an enduring part of the sport and promotional pyrotechnics that have become a model for others to follow.

These are part of the living and indelible legend.

Yet, those of us who were privileged to know him well prefer to remember him as a friend whom we shall never forget.

be fair, he meant a good civic reputation and a history of paying people fairly and on time. The sharp elbows and *Succession*-like drama were added attractions.

Bobby and Jerry Christy in Stampede Wrestling. Photo by Bob Leonard

For his part, Boesch said he almost waited too long to buy the promotion. "I lost a friend, a benefactor, my employer and a man whose decision to employ me had a most profound effect on my life. For 20 years, I had spent my life involved in the everyday details of promotion in Houston," he wrote in his autobiography. "Yet, I had never entertained any thoughts of promoting in Houston. I felt that my close association with Morris called for a high degree of loyalty to him and I supplied it without question. I also knew that wrestling, and the promotion of it, was his life and that despite his prolonged illness, he would be the promoter until the day he died. I could not imagine myself preparing for something that would require the death of a good friend to become an actuality.

"That attitude, as naive as it must seem, almost cost me the opportunity to promote," Boesch continued. "I believed it was proper to observe a definite period of respectful silence and not broach a matter of business to Mrs. Sigel during her bereavement. Yet her phone was ringing from many areas of the coun-

The 55 Year Career of Paul Boesch

try where a different sense of value prevailed. Finally, this gracious lady whose sense of loyalty was much like my own, approached me and told me I had better make my move or someone else would."

In 1959, not long before the San Antonio skirmish, Dizzy Davis, now calling himself a "Personnel Consulting Psychologist," wrote Pfefer ("Director of the Pachyderms") with this observation: "San Antonio is the only city in the state that showed a gain over last year. Of course you will find out why when you get down here. He, the promoter in San Antonio, allows no silly stuff, such as, the loser eating a can of dog food in the ring, riding a jackass down the street, taking a bath in the middle of the ring in a bath-tub, of course, you will think this is all a lie, but down here in Boeschville (as you will learn) this thing is being done every week."

Boesch famously had issues with the Dallas office that ultimately led him to break off from the Southwest Sports booking office. NWA World champion Harley Race no showed a couple of matches, the second one deliberately as pay-

Bill Watts would find success in the ring and promoting, not in football. Department of Special Collections, University Libraries of Notre Dame

back for Boesch leaving the Dallas circuit. This led to Boesch resigning his NWA membership.

In 1981, he partnered with Blanchard to use San Antonio wrestlers on his cards. In 1982, Boesch sold a part of the promotion to Nick Bockwinkel, the American Wrestling Association champion. The San Antonio partnership began when Wahoo McDaniel, the biggest star in Houston history, was booking the South Texas loop. When McDaniel left San Antonio, business went down. Boesch's first wife, Eleonore, died, his health was bothering him, and Birkholz was pitching the idea of making Houston a non-weekly town. The result was a restart May 24, 1982, with a record 11,243 fans at the Sam Houston Coliseum. One of the big draws on the show was the Junkyard Dog, star of the neighboring Mid South Wrestling.

According to *Wrestling Observer Newsletter* publisher Dave Meltzer, Mid South promoter Bill Watts used JYD's success to leverage himself into the Houston promotion. Boesch's version is the booking switches in San Antonio and

STERLING B. DAVIS. PH. D.

PERSONNEL CONSULTING PSYCHOLOGIST

San Antonio is the only city in the state that showed a gain over last year. Of course you will find out why when you get down here. He, the promoter in San Antonio, allows no silly stuff, such as, the loser eating a can of dog food in the ring, riding a jackass down the street, taking a bath in the middle of the ring in a bath-tub. Of course, you think this is all a lie, but down here in Boeschville (As you will learn) this sort of thing is being done every week.

Of course we all feel a bit of vanity or conceit concerning our ability, which I naturally do also, but I could make this territory go within 3 months back to its old level. The boys write me every day, from all over the U. S. A. wanting to know when they can come in for me. They absolutely refuse to come in under the present set-up.

Well Napoleon, when you are ready for the REVOLUTION, let me know !

Dizzy

"TO SAVE YOU VALUABLE TIME

...LE OF RENDERING ANY APTITUDE TEST YOU MAY WISH, WHETHER IT BE ABSTRACT, SOCIAL

Credits:

1) March 13, 1959, Sterling "Dizzy" Davis letter to Jack Pfefer. Davis, now billing himself as a PhD, is on San Antonio's side of its dispute with Houston. Courtesy of the Rare Books and Special Collections Department, Hesburgh Libraries, University of Notre Dame

STERLING B. DAVIS, PH. D.

PERSONNEL CONSULTING PSYCHOLOGIST

Director of the Pachyderms:

Yours received and must report that the territory here has gone steadily down since McShane and myself needled it up a few weeks past.

Some of the boys are working five nites a week and doing from $90.00 to $130.00 per week.

The main event in Houston this Friday, the 17th is Bull Curry versus Joey Maxim the former light heavy boxing champ, in a wrestling match. Maxim refereed here last week in a match between Curry and McShane for the angle for this week.

As for Amarillo, I cannot help but think that Doc is deliberately trying to kill it so his partner, Judge Bartlett can be bought out cheap. My reason for saying this is because the Judge does not know the first principle concerning wrestling, and we both know that Doc is too smart a manipulator to pull what he is pulling, unless it is a deliberate process of killing the territory. Of course, it could be that Doc is just getting old. The things that are done up there would insult the intelligence of an infant.

Give 'em hell, Jack !

"Diz"

Credits:
1) April 15, 1959, Sterling "Dizzy" Davis letter to Jack Pfefer. Courtesy of the Rare Books and Special Collections Department, Hesburgh Libraries, University of Notre Dame

Joe Blanchard's reliance on his son, Tully, made it impossible to continue doing business with Southwest. When Watts offered to bring his hot Mid South product into town instead, it was a partnership that worked for both promoters, at least for a few years.

In August 1982, The Best of Texas Wrestling Inc. replaced the promotion Julius Sigel started in 1925, the Gulf Athletic Club. In September 1982, Watts officially joined the partnership. Birkholz bought out Bockwinkel, whose dream of owning his own territory was crushed by the changes in the business. Southwest stopped sending its talent to Houston by the end of the year and tried to promote in opposition at the basketball arena, The Summit, in May 1983, with disasterous results.

Houston experienced a couple of its best years promoting as a bi-weekly town. However, from 1930 to 1981, the Gulf Athletic Club ran about 50 weeks a year, or more than 2,500 wrestling shows in Houston.

Doc Sarpolis couldn't stay out of the wrestling business. The motel business just didn't compare. Despite his efforts in Dallas and Los Angeles against the NWA, Sarpolis maintained good relationships with the power people, in Texas and in St. Louis. When Dory Detton started having battles with other promoters in the West Texas and Southwest loop, Sarpolis bought the promotion. In 1955, the papers reported Sarpolis paid $75,000 "cash" for what we now call the

HOUSTON VS DALLAS

All-Out 'War' Seen In Texas Wrestling

MORRIS SIGEL

A Promoter and Believer in Clean Sports

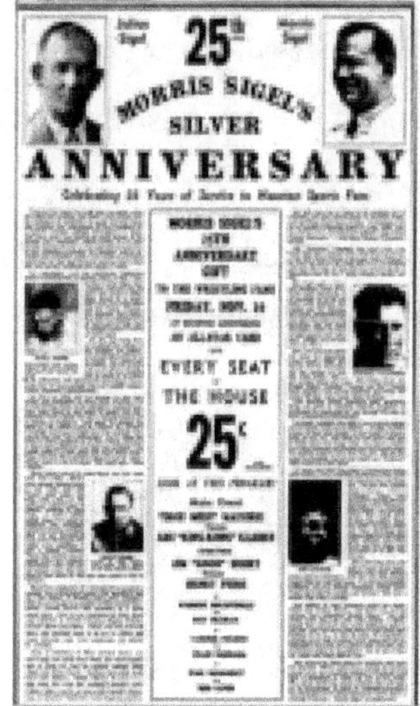

MARCH OF DIMES BENEFIT AT SPORTATORIUM

TONIGHT—JANUARY 28

TEXAS HEAVYWEIGHT CHAMPIONSHIP

PRIZES • PRIZES • PRIZES

Morris Sigel, Houston promoter:
1) Houston Post, Dec. 31, 1930
2) Houston Chronicle, Nov, 9, 1939

Ed McLemore, Dallas promoter:
1) Dallas Morning News, Jan. 25, 1951
2) Dallas Morning News, Jan. 28, 1958

Amarillo territory. Actually, Sarpolis almost moved the headquarters to Lubbock. More importantly, he took on Dork Funk Sr. as his partner, and promoted Gene Kiniski and Dory Funk Jr. as world champions before they won the NWA World Heavyweight title.

Davis went to work for Sarpolis in the Amarillo office. He got fired for allegedly stealing money. In the 1959 letter to Pfefer he wrote, "I was having breakfast with three promoters as to why I left Doc. Now pay attention to this ... each one of them (all three) had been told by Doc that I had stolen from $5,000, $5,800 to $20,000. NONE OF THEM HAD BEEN TOLD THE SAME AMOUNT! So, now the real truth is about to be exposed. Oh well. The hell with it. I have finally accomplished what I set out to do in a different business."

Dr. Sterling Blake Davis, with a "PhD from a University in Mexico" made his debut in the late 1950s. It was a gimmick, but it wasn't a wrestling gimmick. Davis worked as a therapist in the Dallas area for years, only getting exposed because of the prison break and other criminal endeavors, such as a scam to sell bull-frog farm starter kits. Episode 78 of *Greg Klein's Old School Rasslin' Talk*, "Escape from Piedras Negras," talks about the 1976 jail break and the Dr. Davis part of his life.

Tommy "Your Boy Izzy" Phelps got married in 1955 to a civilian. They had kids and she impressed upon him the wickedness of his ways in wrestling. By the early 1960s, Phelps had been converted. He was working for Sarpolis in the Amarillo office, but that ended when he got too preachy. In a letter to Jack Pfefer Nov. 14, 1962, Sarpolis summed it up: "Dear friend Jack, I opened your letter to Izzy and sent it on to him. He is not with us anymore, or did you know? We had to let him go because he became another Karl Davis or Lou Plumber. A PREACHER. Enough said."

By the mid-1960s the former Nature Boy turned revival minister was using his fame to make the rounds on another circuit. Among the revelations he discussed in his ministering, his father was abusive and Izzy often had to stop the man from hurting his mother. Her health concerns in 1953 faded some, and she lived to see her grand babies, as well as her son's transition to the pulpit.

Sarpolis died six months after Sigel, following a heart attack in the aftermath of a boat accident. The Funk boys bought his shares in Amarillo and the promotion gained an outsized reputation for its influence in the NWA and in wrestling overall.

Ironically, Sigel, Sarpolis and McLemore were all eclipsed by their proteges. Paul Boesch, Dory Funk Sr. and Fritz Von Erich are synonymous with Houston, Amarillo and Dallas wrestling. Their territories and towns were shaped by their mentors, whose families all but handed over the wrestling promotions to the apprentices. Yet, the newer generation are given some, most or all of the credit for the success of those promotions. Boesch, Funk Sr. and Von Erich are in pretty much every wrestling Hall of Fame you can find, but Sigel and McLemore are forgotten promoters. The same could be said for Dorathy Livengood and Frank Brown. Their story is mostly forgotten while Joe Blanchard and his son, Tully, have been widely celebrated for the success of the San Antonio promotion and its brief spot in the national spotlight. And in the case of Doc Sarpolis, he is remembered more as a guy who wrestled Strangler Lewis, or the matchmaker who gave us blading, than he is as the man who established Amarillo as an important place on the wrestling map. That credit often goes to Funk Sr. Or it goes to his sons. In the *Wrestling Observer Newsletter* Hall of Fame, Von Erich, Boesch and the Funks are members. Sigel, McLemore, Sarpolis, Livengood and Brown are not in that Hall of Fame.

Still, the history of Texas Rasslin', from the late 1920s to the late 1960s, was dominated by Sigel, Sarpolis, McLemore, Livengood and Brown, and all their associates. The history of Texas wrestling didn't end in the 1950s, but the 1950s set the tone for everything that followed in the next three decades. Long after Sigel, Sarpolis and McLemore had died, the wrestling promotions and the Texas loop they had set up survived and thrived, and the gimmicks they created or imported were still being used. At times, Texas even became the center of the wrestling world.

The promoters of the early territory era in Texas Rasslin' are largely forgotten, but from the Texas style to the Texas title, their work lived on long after them. Their love of wrestling infused Texas with a version of the sport as big as the state. The circuit they created covered some of the biggest cities in America. The era they created, of weekly matches and territory wrestling, no longer exists, except in our memories and imaginations. However, as this story demonstrates, their stories and their legacies are fascinating.

Texas Rasslin' as we knew it wouldn't have existed without them.

RADIO-TELEVISION RECORDING STARS

SONNY JAMES — ROZENA EADS
JOHNNY CARROLL — THE BELEW'S
EDDY McDUFF — BILL DANE

UNDER PERSONAL MANAGEMENT

ED McLEMORE

Cadiz and Industrial Blvd. Riverside 8-4374 Dallas, Texas

Have you noticed the swing is to → "TEXAS RASSLIN"

NO MURDERS!!

NO GUNS!!

NO QUIZZES!!

WE DO HAVE HEROES and VILLAINS in terrific fast ACTION!

FOR NEW REALISTIC PRICES AND AUDITIONS — PHONE, WIRE OR WRITE

MAURICE (MAURY) BECK
Riverside 8-2083 or Riverside 8-3261
Cadiz & Industrial Blvd.
Dallas, Texas

New Lighting—New Angles—New Dimensions—First Runs & Reruns

★ TWELFTH ★ ANNIVERSARY ★

RASSLIN'

Vol. V. No. 13 | Dallas, Texas, Tuesday, January 30, 1951 | Price 10c

TONIGHT Ed McLEMORE OBSERVES HIS TWELFTH ANNIVERSARY OF PROMOTING WRESTLING IN DALLAS!

YOU'RE TH' STAR O' THIS CARD, KID!

THIS ANNIVERSARY PROGRAM IS DEDICATED TO, AND ALL PROCEEDS WILL GO TO THE MARCH OF DIMES!

DURING THESE DOZEN YEARS McLEMORE NOT ONLY HAS BROUGHT THE CHAMPS TO DALLAS --- BUT THE BIG-NAME MAT ATTRACTIONS AS WELL!

WHAT I DO FOR SWEET CHARITY!

McLEMORE'S SHOWS NOT ONLY HELP THE MARCH OF DIMES BUT ALSO CONTRIBUTE TO OTHER CHARITABLE CAUSES!

DALLAS
FT. WORTH
ABILENE
GALVESTON
CORPUS CHRISTI

UNDER THE PROMOTIONAL GUIDANCE OF McLEMORE DALLAS IS THE NO. 1 WRESTLING CITY OF TEXAS!

Credits:

1) Jan. 30, 1951, Dallas program for Ed McLemore's 12th Anniversary. Courtesy of the Rare Books and Special Collections Department, Hesburgh Libraries, University of Notre Dame

Credits:

1) Jan. 29, 1952, Dallas program for Ed McLemore's 13th Anniversary. Courtesy of the Rare Books and Special Collections Department, Hesburgh Libraries, University of Notre Dame

About the Author

Photo by Cheyenne Phillips

The film commissioner for Film Otsego in Cooperstown, New York, Greg Klein is an actor, writer, producer, director and wrestling historian. He was trained to be a professional wrestler by "Exotic" Adrian Street and was mentored by "Golden Boy" Jerry Grey. Listen to Greg Klein's *Old School Rasslin* wherever you get your podcasts.

As an actor, he was on season six of *24* as a Russian henchman and graduated from The Second City's New York City program.

He has published three other books, the biography of the Junkyard Dog, *The King of New Orleans*, the historic fiction baseball novel, *The Paper Tigers*, and a collection of plays, *Sunset Painting & The Sun*.

Follow Greg: X = @JYDBook BlueSky = @jydbook.bsky.social

Instagram = @film_greg and @filmotsego

Facebook = Greg Klein's Old School Rasslin Talk

www.ingramcontent.com/pod-product-compliance
Lightning Source LLC
LaVergne TN
LVHW010615100826
845148LV00014B/2984

* 9 7 8 1 7 3 7 8 6 3 5 2 6 *